OHIO'S
PRESIDENTS

OHIO'S PRESIDENTS

A History & Guide

HEATHER S. COLE

THE
History
PRESS

Published by The History Press
Charleston, SC
www.historypress.com

First published 2024

Manufactured in the United States

ISBN 9781467156530

Library of Congress Control Number: 2024930893

To my parents, Kevin and Barbara O'Connor,
with thanks for their encouragement of my writing for all these years.

CONTENTS

ACKNOWLEDGEMENTS

Although I grew up elsewhere, I have roots in the Buckeye State: my paternal great-great-grandfather ran a religious goods store in Toledo, and two generations of his descendants grew up there. My maternal grandfather worked in the General Motors plant in Lordstown, and I spent many holidays and long weekends throughout my childhood visiting the home he shared with my grandmother in Boardman.

It has been delightful to return to Ohio as an adult and fill in the gaps in my knowledge about Ohio history and, specifically, the Ohio-born U.S. presidents. Along the way, I have met many wonderful tour guides, museum educators and Ohio boosters who have helped me with my research. They include Heather Bowman, Colette Broestler, Sandra M. Cobb, Brian Dettelbach, Maureen Geck, Michelle Gullion, Sherry Hall, Kimberly A. Kenney, Stephanie Macklin, Anne E. Marshall, Brett McCrery, Dustin McLochlin, Geoffrey Mendelsohn, Greg Roberts, Jenni Salamon, Kristina Smith, Holly Sukol, Neil Thompson, Noah Tjijenda, Christie Weininger and Belinda Weiss. Thank you to all of them and the rest of the staff and volunteers at the museums, presidential libraries and historic sites across Ohio. I would also like to express my appreciation to my travel companion, Barbara O'Connor; my editor, John Rodrigue; the staff at The History Press; and my beta readers Josh Cole, Camille Dierksheide and David Dierksheide for their valuable contributions to this book. Any remaining mistakes are my own.

Presidential sites in Ohio. *Created by Caroline Rodrigues.*

INTRODUCTION

Ohio's Presidents: A History & Guide is the second in a series of books designed to provide an overview of the lives of the U.S. presidents and a handy reference to the museums, historic homes and presidential libraries that tell their stories. Written for the casual reader, these books do not attempt to replicate the extensive scholarship on the U.S. presidents. Instead, it is my hope that they will provide enough background information on the presidents to better enjoy visits to their homes and museums and whet the reader's appetite to learn more.

The first book in this series, *Virginia's Presidents: A History & Guide*, was published by The History Press in 2023 and covers the eight U.S. presidents born in the Old Dominion: George Washington, Thomas Jefferson, James Madison, James Monroe, William Henry Harrison, John Tyler, Zachary Taylor and Woodrow Wilson. *Virginia's Presidents* was conceived while I was working as a tour guide at the Woodrow Wilson Presidential Library and Museum in Staunton, Virginia, and would regularly encounter visitors who were spending their holidays visiting presidential homes and libraries across the state and beyond. In providing recommendations to them on other places to visit, I discovered that there was no guide to the homes and museums of Virginia presidents that was still in print. It seemed like a niche needing to be filled. I spent 2022 researching and writing, and *Virginia's Presidents* was published the following January.

Like many of the visitors I encountered as a tour guide, I discovered that U.S. presidential history can be a bit addictive. As I gave talks at libraries and historical societies to promote *Virginia's Presidents*, I continued to hear recommendations on presidential sites across the country that I had not yet visited, including several in Ohio. A friend's husband raved about the home of Rutherford B. Hayes in Freemont, and a colleague told me about the innovative model adopted by the McKinley Presidential Library and Museum in Canton. I did some reading, visited a few Ohio presidential sites and had to admit that I was hooked. I spent 2023 conducting research and visiting (and revisiting) historic sites across the Buckeye State. The book in your hands is the result.

FIVE DECADES IN A CHANGING AMERICA

Ohio is the birthplace of seven U.S. presidents, more than any other state in the Union except Virginia. (Virginia-born William Henry Harrison, claimed by both Ohio and Virginia, is included in *Virginia's Presidents: A History & Guide.*) Their presidencies were clustered in a five-decade period between 1869 and 1923, arguably one of the most transformative periods in U.S. history.

During this period, the United States more than doubled its population—from 39 million to 106 million people, including more than 20 million immigrants, largely from southern and eastern Europe. The great migration west that had begun before the Civil War continued, and in 1890, the U.S. Census Bureau announced that there was no land left in the United States that had not been settled. By 1912, the remaining territories on the continental United States had been neatly divided into states and accepted into the Union, bringing the number of stars on Old Glory to forty-eight. (Alaska and Hawaii would become states in 1959.) The United States officially now reached "from sea to shining sea."

These fifty years were also a time of rapid social and economic change. From its beginnings, most Americans lived on farms and in small villages; by 1920, the federal census reported that a majority of Americans lived in urban areas—5.5 million in New York City alone. Many of these people came to the cities to find work, living in overcrowded tenements and laboring long days in dangerous and unregulated factories for less than a living wage. Yet this was also a period of great wealth for a small number of businessmen and industrialists as American factories implemented new technology to streamline operations and found buyers for U.S. products abroad. This widening gap between the rich and the poor would eventually lead to efforts in the early twentieth century—including by some of the Ohio presidents—to regulate business monopolies and provide basic social services to the needy.

When the first Ohio-born president took office in 1869, the United States was still navigating Reconstruction and trying to rebuild a union without relying on the labor of enslaved people. By the time the last Buckeye president died in office in 1923, suffrage had been extended to both formerly enslaved people and women. While there was still rampant racism, sexism and nativism throughout the country, the stage was set for some of the larger political and social reforms that would follow later in the twentieth century.

As chief executives, the seven Ohio presidents presided over these five decades of change across the United States. Their leadership helped chart a course that transformed a young nation, traumatized and divided by Civil War, into a powerful leader on the world stage.

THE BUCKEYE PRESIDENTS

The Buckeye presidents range from the celebrated to the obscure. Most notable among the former is our eighteenth president, Ulysses S. Grant. Although he is usually remembered for his role as commanding general of Union forces during the Civil War, Grant later served two terms in the White House, from 1869 to 1877. During that time, he worked to rebuild the schism between North and South and advocated for the rights of freed slaves.

Among the lesser-known presidents was Grant's successor, Rutherford B. Hayes, who served one term in office from 1877 to 1881. Hayes took office following a controversial election that traded Electoral College votes for a promise to withdraw the remaining federal troops from the South, ending Reconstruction. As president, Hays advocated for civil service reform and funding for public education.

Another single-term president was number twenty-three: Benjamin Harrison. Grandson of the ninth president and great-grandson of a signer of the Declaration of Independence, Harrison served in the executive office from 1889 to 1893. He advocated for high tariffs to protect American business interests while also signing into law legislation that would limit the growth of business monopolies.

Two Ohio presidents had their time in the White House cut short by assassins' bullets. James A. Garfield, our twentieth president, had plans to expand international trade and introduce federally funded public education, but he was shot in July 1881, after just six months in office. Our twenty-fifth president, William McKinley, took office in 1897. He led the United States to victory in the Spanish-American War and was expanding America's influence in Asia when he was killed in September 1901, six months into his second term.

McKinley's vice president was the dynamic New Yorker Teddy Roosevelt, who served two terms and then handpicked his successor, Ohioan William Howard Taft. Taft served one term (1909–13), during which he worked to streamline the functioning of the federal government and promoted U.S. business interests abroad. But Taft was not the progressive reformer that Roosevelt had hoped, so Roosevelt ran against him in the 1912 presidential election, splitting the Republican vote and giving Virginia-born Democrat Woodrow Wilson the White House.

The last Ohio-born president (to date) was newspaperman Warren G. Harding. Our twenty-ninth president was elected in 1921 on a campaign promise to "return to normalcy" after the First World War. Harding worked for greater oversight of the federal budget and advocated for a postwar reduction in the military. He died of a presumed heart attack two years into his presidency.

A few generalizations can be made about the men whom Ohio sent to the White House. All seven were Republicans, in a period when the Republican Party was the one that supported civil rights, protection of U.S. business interests and, after the turn of the twentieth century, progressive social movements. They were all married men in their late forties to mid-fifties with children or stepchildren. The first five Ohio presidents had all served in the Union army during the Civil War. Most of them had worked as attorneys and had previous political experience in the Ohio legislature and Congress prior to election to the presidency. They made major decisions that had long-lasting impact on the future of the United States and the world, but they also cared for ill wives, mourned their children's deaths and sometimes struggled to pay the bills.

Ohio also had a few presidential firsts. The Buckeye State was home to the first "front porch" presidential campaign strategy, which invited selected supporters to the candidate's home for carefully choreographed events, rather than traveling the country giving speeches. Three Ohio presidents made successful use of this strategy. When Black people and women cast their votes for president for the first time, they elected Ohioans to the executive office. Ohio presidents made the first phone call from the White House, hosted the first Easter Egg Roll and listened to the radio for the first time from the executive mansion.

OHIO PRESIDENTIAL SITES

From Canton to Fremont and Mentor to North Bend, nearly two dozen historic sites across Ohio and beyond interpret the lives of the seven Buckeye presidents. They include presidential birthplaces, libraries, memorials and museums. Visitors can take guided tours of presidential homes, participate in living history programs, conduct research in museum archives and even listen to an animatronic presidential storyteller.

Many of the sites in Ohio are part of the Ohio History Connection, a statewide organization that manages more than fifty historic sites. Others are part of the National Park Service system or are independently operated by dedicated nonprofit organizations and passionate local historians. All offer tours and interpretation for both the presidential history buff and the casual visitor, and many also have programs and activities for children, particularly during summer and school holidays.

Some of the presidential sites also tell stories beyond the presidents: the James A. Garfield National Historic Site tells the story of Lucretia Garfield and her work to preserve her husband's legacy; the First Ladies National Historic Site tells the story of Ida McKinley and other first ladies; and the McKinley Presidential Library and Museum places its namesake president squarely in the context of local social and economic history.

Big or small, these presidential sites are an important contribution to our cultural landscape, and their exhibits, tours and educational programs allow us to better understand the people who helped shape the nation we have today.

ULYSSES S. GRANT

OUR EIGHTEENTH PRESIDENT

FAST FACTS ABOUT ULYSSES S. GRANT

- Eighteenth president of the United States
- Born on April 27, 1822; died on July 23, 1885
- Served two terms: 1869–77
- Married Julia Dent (1826–1902) in 1848
- Children: Frederick Dent (1850–1912), Ulysses Simpson (1852–1929), Ellen Wrenshall (1855–1922) and Jesse Root (1858–1934)
- Signed the bill creating Yellowstone National Park, the first national park in the United States
- Face is on the fifty-dollar bill
- Owned one enslaved person and freed him in 1859
- Prior careers: military officer, farmer, store clerk

ALL ABOUT ULYSSES S. GRANT

Ulysses S. Grant is best remembered as a hero general of the Civil War, leading the United States to victory over the Confederacy. He was at his best in the heat of battle: calm, courageous and skilled at military strategy.

Ulysses S. Grant, circa
1869–77. *Photograph by
Mathew B. Brady. Library
of Congress, Prints and
Photographs Division.*

When he was elected eighteenth president of the United States and stepped
into office in 1869, he brought with him a general's demeanor—expecting
loyalty, dedication and duty to nation from his staff. During his first term,
he oversaw the former Confederate states' return to the Union, fought to
protect the rights of freedmen and worked to stabilize the postwar U.S.
economy. However, Grant's presidency was also marred by political scandal,
as several members of his administration were accused of taking bribes, and
his reputation suffered in the years that followed.

EARLY LIFE

Hiram Ulysses Grant was born on April 27, 1822 in Point Pleasant, Ohio,
a small village about twenty-five miles southeast of Cincinnati along the
Ohio River. It was, at the time, the western frontier of the still-young United
States of America. Ulysses, as he was known, was the first child born to

Hannah Simpson Grant and Jesse Grant. Jesse had grown up in poverty and was apprenticed out to work on local farms from the age of eleven. He was eventually taken in by the father of abolitionist John Brown, who mentored Jesse in both the tannery business and in abolitionism. By the age of twenty-six, Jesse was working as a foreman at a tannery in Point Pleasant, where he met Hannah Simpson, the daughter of a local farmer. Ulysses was born ten months after their marriage.

By the time Ulysses was a year old, Jesse had saved enough money to open his own tannery. The family moved thirty miles east to Georgetown, Ohio, another small rural southern Ohio community, where Jesse built a two-story brick house across the street from the tannery. Ulysses was raised here with three younger sisters and two younger brothers. He attended a two-room schoolhouse just a half-mile walk from home until the age of fourteen.

Ulysses was good at mathematics but more interested in horsemanship than his studies. Although unsure of his future, Ulysses was determined not to enter his father's tannery businesses, which he considered dirty and smelly. Jesse, too, wished better things for his eldest son and scraped together the funds to send Ulysses to private school for two terms in hopes that it would prepare him for the U.S. Military Academy at West Point. At the time, West Point was the best option in higher education for a family that could not otherwise afford college: a free education in exchange for military service.

Hiram Ulysses Grant grew up in this home in Georgetown, Ohio, and attended a two-room schoolhouse nearby. *Photograph by Nick Cole.*

Then—as now—admission to West Point was very competitive and required a congressional nomination. Jesse received word that another local boy had dropped out of West Point and, seizing the opportunity, applied for Ulysses's admittance on his behalf. When the nominating congressman completed paperwork for Ulysses, he mistakenly substituted Ulysses's mother's maiden name—Simpson—for his legal one. Ulysses never bothered to correct the error, and he was subsequently known as Ulysses S. Grant.

When Ulysses enrolled at West Point in 1839, he was seventeen years old, five feet eleven inches and all of 117 pounds. He was a shy, quiet student who did well in mathematics but only acceptable in his other coursework. He also did not seem to embrace the pomp and circumstance of a military school, only tolerating the marching and drills that were a part of daily cadet life. He was recognized, however, for his horsemanship and hoped desperately to be commissioned into the cavalry after graduation. He was not selected, but after graduation, he was instead commissioned into the Fourth Infantry Regiment and shipped off to St. Louis, Missouri. And thus began Grant's military career.

EARLY CAREER

The best thing to come out of Ulysses S. Grant's early military career was his marriage. The Fourth Infantry Regiment was based in the Jefferson Barracks near St. Louis, Missouri. Ulysses's roommate from West Point had grown up on a plantation nearby, and his parents opened their home to the former cadets. On one such visit, Ulysses met and was immediately taken with eighteen-year-old Julia Dent. The couple would have a long engagement, in part because of family differences—the Dents thought that Julia should marry someone of her social standing; the Grants didn't approve of the slaveholding Dents—and in part because Ulysses was soon called away to fight in the Mexican-American War.

In 1845, the United States annexed Texas as the twenty-eighth state in the Union. However, there was lingering conflict with Mexico over the location of the southern border of Texas, and President James Polk pressured Mexico to sell the land that would eventually become the American Southwest. Negotiations between the United States and Mexico deteriorated over the next several months. In April 1846, following a battle that broke out between U.S. and Mexican troops along the Rio Grande, Congress declared war.

Ulysses S. Grant and his family, circa 1868. *Original painting by William Cogswell, engraving by John Sartain. Library of Congress, Prints and Photographs Division.*

The Fourth Infantry Regiment, including Grant, was sent to the Texas border and then served under the command of General (and future U.S. president) Zachary Taylor. When war broke out, they crossed into Mexico, and Grant saw action in the battles of Palo Alto, Resaca de la Palma and

Monterrey. He served as regimental quartermaster for a time, where he learned the logistics of supplying an army, something that would serve him well during the Civil War. He was recognized for his bravery, including an incident when he rode past snipers to deliver a message, hanging off the side of his horse.

It was during the Mexican-American War that Grant began to see a future for himself in the military. Although he hated being away from Julia—and married her as soon as he could get leave after war's end—he found that he was preternaturally calm and focused in the heat of battle and that the strategic planning of war suited his mathematical mind. Unfortunately, he found the mundaneness of peacetime in the military to be excruciating.

Initially, Julia was able to follow him as the military moved Ulysses around the country as needs demanded. But when he was sent to the West Coast in 1852, Julia was pregnant with their second child, and the trip was deemed too dangerous. In those long months away from his family, and perhaps suffering from depression, Grant began drinking alcohol to excess. Following a warning from his commanding officer, Grant resigned from the U.S. Army in the summer of 1854. He was thirty-two years old, a married father of two with another on the way and needed a new job.

The Grant family moved to White Haven, Julia's family's plantation outside St. Louis, Missouri. The couple had been given eighty acres of land as a wedding gift, and they purchased another one thousand acres from the Dents. Ulysses used enslaved labor to build his family a home and tried his hand at farming. The couple had two more children, but Julia hated living in the country and Ulysses was not very good at farming. He was also apparently ambivalent about the nature of southern plantation life and freed the one enslaved person whom he owned, a man named William Jones who had been given to him by his in-laws.

When a nationwide financial crisis hit in 1857 and their finances took a tumble, Ulysses packed up his family and moved into the city of St. Louis. He worked briefly as a rent collector for a Dent cousin but was not terribly successful in that endeavor. By 1860, the Grants were in enough financial trouble that Ulysses was forced to ask his father for a job.

By then, Jesse Grant had expanded his tannery business and owned a leather goods store in Galena, Illinois, where his younger sons also worked. He offered Ulysses a job as a clerk in the shop, and the family of six moved to northwestern Illinois. This was perhaps the lowest point in Ulysses's life: working under the supervision of his younger brothers in his father's shop in an industry that he had forsworn as a child. But he now had four children of his own to support. He hated the work but loved the time with his family.

On April 12, 1861, Grant's life changed, along with thousands of others, when the first shots of the Civil War were fired at Fort Sumter, South Carolina. That summer, Grant was commissioned as colonel in charge of the Twenty-First Illinois Volunteer Infantry Regiment. He was at last back doing the work that he believed he was meant to do.

CIVIL WAR

Much has been written about Ulysses S. Grant's accomplishments during the Civil War, and he is credited with leading the United States to victory over the Confederacy. He had a focused strategic mind, was a skilled communicator and was absolutely unwilling to back down once he had embarked on a plan of action. Although some criticized him for the number of casualties under his command, Grant understood early on in the war that a vast number of men would have to be sacrificed to preserve the Union. And when the South eventually surrendered, he was among the group that argued for restoration of the former Confederate states to the Union, rather than punishment.

After training the Twenty-First Illinois Volunteers in the summer of 1861, Grant was promoted to brigadier general and given command of twenty thousand troops with instructions to provide defense in the western theater of the war. Based on his experience managing supplies in the Mexican-American War, Grant had a good understanding of what was needed to sustain an army. He correctly assessed that the Union could strangle the Confederacy by cutting off their supply routes and eyed the Mississippi River and its various tributaries as targets. By early the next year, Grant had persuaded his superiors to allow him to begin an offensive campaign, and he led his troops to capture Fort Henry and Fort Donelson in northwestern Tennessee, located on the Tennessee and Cumberland Rivers. These were the first important Union victories and earned Grant a promotion to major general over what would shortly be known as the Army of the Tennessee.

In April 1862, Grant came face to face with fellow West Point alumni P.G.T. Beauregard and Albert Sidney Johnston at the Battle of Shiloh when the two Confederates led their Army of Mississippi on an attack on Grant's troops in southwestern Tennessee. Johnston was killed in the conflict, and Beauregard was forced to retreat. Shiloh was a Union strategic victory, but

General Ulysses S. Grant at his Civil War headquarters, 1864. *Photograph by Egbert Guy Fowx. Library of Congress, Prints and Photographs Division.*

both the North and South were shocked by the number of casualties; an estimated twenty thousand were killed or wounded. It was the bloodiest battle up to that time but an important win for the Union.

Later that fall, Grant saw an opportunity to make a significant strike against the Confederacy by going after their fort at Vicksburg, Mississippi.

Troops led by Major General John A. McClernand, Major General William T. Sherman and Grant all made attempts to attack Vicksburg by water. After they were repeatedly beaten back, Grant hatched a plan to maneuver troops south of Vicksburg and attack the fort by land. Along the way, Grant captured the Mississippi capital of Jackson. When his direct attacks on Vicksburg were unsuccessful, Grant staged a military blockade, cutting the city off from supplies and reinforcements. Forty days later, in July 1863, Vicksburg surrendered. This victory was a turning point in the war, as it gave the Union control of the Mississippi River and effectively split the Confederacy in half.

Meanwhile, the Confederate army was holding the Union Army of the Cumberland under siege along the Tennessee River in Chattanooga, Tennessee. President Abraham Lincoln promoted Grant to commander and sent him to Chattanooga. There, Grant combined forces with Sherman, Major General Joseph Hooker and Major General George H. Thomas to resupply the starving Union troops and launched an offensive on the Confederates. Their success in the fall of 1863 gave the Union full control of Tennessee and opened access to Georgia and points deeper into the Confederate South.

After Chattanooga, Grant was promoted to lieutenant general and given command of the entire U.S. Army. He met with Lincoln in the spring of 1864 and devised a plan to defeat the Confederacy finally and totally. Shortly thereafter, Grant launched a campaign against Robert E. Lee's Army of Northern Virginia that chased him around central Virginia while Sherman marched his troops toward Atlanta. What became known as the Overland Campaign would come to comprise the Battles of Wilderness, Spotsylvania and Richmond and resulted in high casualties among the Union troops as Grant refused to let up pressure. Grant's plan eventually worked, and in June 1864, he surrounded Lee's troops in Petersburg, Virginia.

While Grant held the Army of Northern Virginia under siege in Petersburg, Sherman's troops captured Atlanta, and he began his infamous March to the Sea, destroying military and civilian infrastructure as his soldiers made their way across Georgia to the port of Savannah. The Army of the Shenandoah, under the command of General Philip Sheridan, also had successes in western Virginia, Georgia and South Carolina in the fall of 1864. It was becoming clear that there was no path to a Confederate victory, and Lee eventually surrendered his army at Appomattox Court House, Virginia, on April 9, 1865. Although there were a few minor battles after, the Civil War was effectively over.

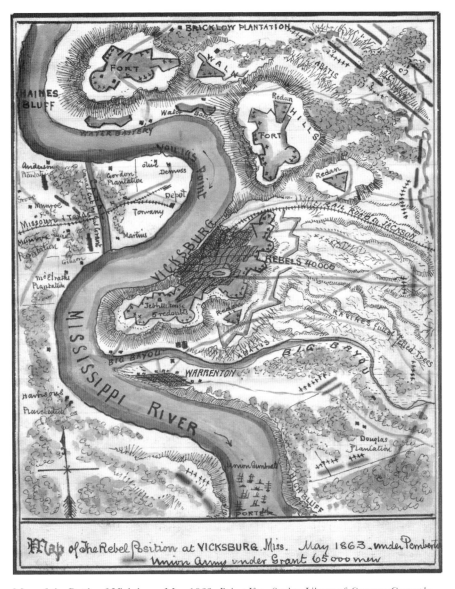

Map of the Battle of Vicksburg, May 1863. *Robert Knox Sneden. Library of Congress, Geography and Map Division.*

Grant was forty-three years old and a war hero credited with saving the Union. After four years of war, there was one last bullet that he narrowly escaped five days later. He and Julia had been invited by President Lincoln to celebrate the end of war by attending a performance of the comedy *Our American Cousin* in Washington, D.C. Julia, who did not get along with Mary

Robert E. Lee surrenders to Ulysses S. Grant at Appomattox Court House, Virginia, on April 9, 1865. *Published by John Smith. Library of Congress, Prints and Photographs Division.*

Todd Lincoln, persuaded Ulysses not to attend. Her decision likely saved his life, as it was on that evening—April 14, 1865—that actor and Confederate sympathizer John Wilkes Booth climbed into the presidential box at Ford's Theatre and shot Lincoln in the back of his head. Later, it would be revealed that Booth and his co-conspirators also planned to kill Grant.

After Lincoln's assassination, President Andrew Johnson promoted Grant to general of the army. Grant also served briefly under Johnson as acting secretary of war, but they conflicted over implementation of Reconstruction, and Grant stepped down after just a few months.

PRESIDENT

Ulysses S. Grant was one in a long line of war heroes elected to the executive office, even though the characteristics and skills that make a great general are not necessarily the same that make a great president. Nevertheless, the Republican National Convention unanimously selected Grant as its presidential candidate when it met in the fall of 1868. His Democratic opponent was former New York governor Horatio Seymour. As was typical of the time, Grant did not campaign, leaving that to other members of his party. Popular among both Blacks and northern whites, Grant won the Electoral College by a landslide 214 to 80 votes and nearly 53 percent of the popular vote. He also carried six of the southern states, thanks in large part to the votes cast by formerly enslaved people.

Grant spent much of his first term in the White House overseeing Reconstruction in the South. He negotiated the readmission of the former Confederate states to the Union and signed the Amnesty Act, which restored voting rights to most of the former Confederates. He advocated for civil rights for freedmen and encouraged the ratification of the Fifteenth Amendment to the U.S. Constitution, which granted voting rights to men of all races. He dispatched the military to fight the Ku Klux Klan and successfully negotiated payment from England for their support of the Confederacy during the Civil War. He had a few stumbles—including a failed attempt to annex Santo Domingo, in part to have a place for freedmen to flee the oppression of the continental South—but was easily reelected president in 1872.

However, by the beginning of Grant's second term, an economic depression had hit. The economic downturn put pressure on the Grant administration to wrap up Reconstruction and move on to pressing financial concerns, specifically reducing the huge national debt generated during the Civil War. Grant also signed legislation that recalled paper currency issued during the war to replace it with currency tied to the gold standard. The hope was that this would stabilize the economy and reduce inflation.

Grant's second term in office also coincided with the beginning of what would come to be known as the Gilded Age—an era of industrialization, rapid economic growth and the concentration of wealth in the North. This is the period that saw the rise of the captains of industry, including John D. Rockefeller, Jay Gould, Andrew Carnegie, Cornelius Vanderbilt and others who would eventually become household names. Political corruption during the Gilded Age was a given. Wealthy men spent untold sums making sure that they could continue to grow their fortunes—and this often included paying bribes to politicians. Grant's administration was not exempt from the graft and political scandal that came to define the era.

Despite his popularity, Grant's battlefield acumen did not translate well to the role of president. He continued to operate as a general, issuing orders rather than engaging in the negotiations, consultations and compromises required in politics. He relied heavily on his subordinates and expected the type of piety that was intrinsic to military structure. He was also trusting to a fault, and when faced with signs of disloyalty and corruption, Grant did not always condemn the perpetrators. Among the scandals of his presidency was the Crédit Mobilier affair of 1872, wherein directors of the Union Pacific Railroad funneled federal money for railroad expansion through a dummy corporation and then paid off Congress in stocks to discourage investigation and a law he signed in 1873 that doubled his own salary. Grant was also criticized for the actions of several of his advisors and appointees, including both his secretary of the treasury and his secretary of war, who were involved in kickback and bribery schemes. Although he was not directly implicated in any of the scandals, they tainted Grant's reputation enough that he decided not to run for a third term.

POST-PRESIDENCY LIFE

Ulysses S. Grant left the White House in March 1877, succeeded by fellow Ohioan Rutherford B. Hayes. Grant and Julia then embarked on what would turn into a two-year-long round-the-world tour. During the tour, he was greeted as a celebrity and feted by political leaders and royalty from England to China.

When the Grants eventually returned to the United States, Ulysses once again found himself unemployed. At the time, there were no pensions for former presidents, and the Grants had spent their savings on their world tour. Wealthy friends bought the couple a house in Manhattan, and Grant embarked on a short-lived partnership to try to build a railroad in Mexico. He attempted a third presidential run in 1880 but lost the Republican nomination to fellow Ohioan James A. Garfield.

In 1883, Grant—demonstrating once again a misplaced trust—made the dubious decision to become a silent partner in his son Ulysses's Wall Street investment firm. It turned out to be a pyramid scheme, and Grant lost nearly all his money, including $150,000 he had borrowed from William Henry Vanderbilt. Grant was forced to sell off his Missouri farm, White Haven, and his house in Galena, Illinois.

Shortly thereafter, Grant was diagnosed with throat cancer—likely caused by years of cigar smoking. It was incurable. At a low point matched only, perhaps, by his time in the West prior to the Civil War, Grant was approached by his friend Samuel Clemens, who suggested that Grant write his memoirs.

Ulysses S. Grant at his home in Mount McGregor, New York, July 1885. *Photograph by John G. Gilman. Library of Congress, Prints and Photographs Division.*

Clemens—better known under his pen name, Mark Twain—promised to publish whatever Grant wrote and assured him that the royalties would be enough to support Julia after his death.

Grant spent the rest of his life writing. He finished his memoir just one week before his death, on July 23, 1885, in New York. He was sixty-three years old. *The Personal Memoirs of Ulysses S. Grant* were published posthumously and earned Julia more than $450,000 in royalties, making it one of the bestselling books of the nineteenth century.

ULYSSES S. GRANT HISTORIC SITES IN OHIO

Ulysses S. Grant Birthplace

1551 State Route 232, Point Pleasant, OH
513-497-0492
ohiohistory.org/visit/browse-historical-sites/u-s-grant-birthplace

Hiram Ulysses Grant, as he was named by his parents, was born in a tiny frontier village along the banks of the Ohio River in 1822. Point Pleasant, as it was then known, was home to Ulysses for just the first year of his life. The family then moved on to Georgetown, Ohio, where Grant spent his childhood.

After Grant's death in 1885, the single-story wood cottage where he was born became a traveling memorial. The house was removed from its original location and shipped down the Ohio River for exhibition in Cincinnati, then moved to Columbus and installed in a specially designed building on the state fairgrounds. Around the 100th anniversary of Grant's birth, a local resident spearheaded the effort to return the home to its original location. In 1936, the house was dismantled and returned to Point Pleasant. Evidence suggests that much of the house was replaced during that final move, although the windows, floorboards and some other elements are believed to be original.

The Ulysses S. Grant Birthplace is currently operated as a historic house museum by the Ohio History Connection and Historic New Richmond Inc.

The home where Hiram Ulysses Grant was born in Point Pleasant, Ohio, traveled across the state in the late nineteenth century and then was reconstructed on the original site where it remains today. *Photograph by Nick Cole.*

The house contains several items that belonged to members of the Grant family, including furniture, clothing and a cigar case given to Grant during his post-presidency around-the-world tour. The birthplace is open seasonally, and an admission is charged.

U.S. Grant Boyhood Home and Schoolhouse
219 East Grant Avenue, Georgetown, OH
877-372-8177
usgrantboyhoodhome.org

When Ulysses was just a year old, the Grant family relocated to Georgetown, Ohio, where his father operated a tannery across the street from their house. Ulysses lived in this home until he left to enroll at West Point at the age of seventeen. The one-and-a-half-story Federal-style brick house is currently interpreted to 1839, the year that Grant left home, and includes some original furniture. There is also a small exhibit about Grant's life.

A half mile from his boyhood home is the two-room schoolhouse that Grant attended from 1829 to 1835. The schoolhouse contains an original bench believed to be used by Grant and a small exhibit.

The U.S. Grant Boyhood Home and Schoolhouse are Ohio History Connection sites and managed locally by the Ulysses S. Grant Homestead Association. The museums are open seasonally, and an admission is charged that includes both sites.

ULYSSES S. GRANT HISTORIC SITES OUTSIDE OF OHIO

Ulysses S. Grant National Historic Site
7400 Grant Road, St. Louis, MO
314-842-1867
nps.gov/ulsg

Ulysses S. Grant met his future wife, Julia Dent, at her family home, White Haven, while stationed at the nearby Jefferson Barracks early in his military career. When Ulysses married Julia in 1848, the son of an abolitionist married into a family of slaveholders. Initially, the couple lived with the

Dents at White Haven, and Ulysses helped manage the enslaved people there—owning at least one enslaved person whom he eventually freed. After the Civil War, Ulysses purchased White Haven from his father-in-law. He hired a caretaker and made many upgrades to the property, including the construction of a horse stable, with plans to retire there. However, the couple never lived at White Haven full time, settling in New York City instead. In 1885, the Grants were forced to sell White Haven to pay off the debts Ulysses accumulated by investing in his son's failed Wall Street firm.

After the Grants lost White Haven, it passed through several owners, including one who tried to convert the estate into an amusement park. It was first open for tours in 1913, while still in private hands. In the 1980s, the estate was under threat of private development, and a nonprofit organization was formed to try to save it. The land was eventually acquired by the National Park Service, which operates it today.

The Ulysses S. Grant National Historic Site is composed of the Dent home and outbuildings, a visitor center and museum. The house is open by guided tour; the museum is self-guided. The site is open daily, and admission is free.

Grant's Farm

10501 Gravois Road, St. Louis, MO
314-843-1700
grantsfarm.com

After Ulysses S. Grant and Julia Dent were married, Julia's father gave them eighty acres of land from White Haven, his plantation southwest of St. Louis, Missouri. In 1856, the Grants built a small cabin on their land and named it Hardscrabble. They were not particularly successful in farming, and an economic depression hit soon after. The Grants sold the sixty acres around Hardscrabble and moved to Illinois for Ulysses to take a job working in his father's leather goods store.

In 1903, the CEO of beer company Anheuser-Busch purchased the land that had belonged to Grant and named it Grant's Farm. The same year, another wealthy businessman purchased Hardscrabble and moved it to St. Louis to put on display for the 1904 World's Fair. A few years later, the Anheuser-Busch CEO purchased Hardscrabble and returned it to Grant's Farm, placing it about a mile from where it originally stood. In the 1950s, the Busch family opened Grant's Farm to the public.

Grant's Farm is adjacent to the Ulysses S. Grant National Historic Site. It is owned and operated by Anheuser-Busch and is open daily as an animal preserve and event space. General admission is free, but a fee is charged for parking and a behind-the-scenes tour of Hardscrabble.

Ulysses S. Grant Home State Historic Site

500 Bouthillier Street, Galena, IL
815-777-3310
granthome.org

Ulysses S. Grant first moved his family to Galena, Illinois, in 1860 after his failed attempts at farming and other endeavors in the St. Louis area. While there, the family rented a small house and Grant worked in the leather goods store owned by his father. The family was in Galena just a year before Grant left to fight in the Civil War. At the end of the war, Grant returned to Galena a hero. A group of local Republicans purchased this Italianate-style brick house for $2,500 and gave it to Grant. This was just the first of many generous donations the Grants would receive over the years.

After Grant was elected president, the house was maintained by caretakers, and he visited only occasionally. After his death, his children donated the house to the City of Galena as a memorial to their father. It was eventually turned over to the State of Illinois and restored to its 1868 appearance.

The Ulysses S. Grant Home is open by guided tour Wednesday through Sunday, and an admission is charged.

Ulysses S. Grant Cottage State Historic Site

1000 Mount McGregor Road, Wilton, NY
518-584-4353
grantcottage.org

The Grants moved to Wilton, New York, in June 1885 so that Ulysses could have the time and space to finish writing his memoirs. They moved into a cottage adjacent to Hotel Balmoral, a mountain resort. Grant was sick with throat cancer and finished his writing just days before his death on July 23, 1885.

After Grant's death, the property was preserved as a historic site with a local caretaker and was open for visitors upon request. In 1989, a friends group took over management and continues to operate the site today. Visitors to the cottage tour the downstairs, including original furnishings and personal items.

The Ulysses S. Grant Cottage is open seasonally, and an admission is charged.

General Grant National Monument
Riverside Drive and West 122nd Street, New York, NY
646-670-7251
nps.gov/gegr

After her husband's death, Julia Grant selected Riverside Park in New York City as the location for his entombment, as she believed it would be a convenient location for both her and his admirers to visit. Ulysses was interred in a temporary tomb while plans were drawn up for a permanent memorial. Eventually, more than $600,000 in donations were raised to build this granite and marble structure. It is the largest mausoleum in North America

Grant's Tomb and Riverside Park in New York City, circa 1900. *Published by Detroit Photographic Co. Library of Congress, Prints and Photographs Division.*

and includes 143-foot ceilings, mosaic murals depicting Grant during the Civil War and carvings representing phases of his life. The monument was dedicated in 1897 on the seventy-fifth anniversary of Grant's birth.

The General Grant National Monument includes the mausoleum and a visitor center. It is open Wednesday through Sunday, and admission is free.

Ulysses S. Grant Presidential Library

Mississippi State University, Mitchell Memorial Library, 395 Hardy Boulevard, Starkville, MS
662-325-4552
usgrantlibrary.org/museum

The Ulysses S. Grant Presidential Library houses correspondence, photographs and artifacts relating to Grant and is open to researchers by appointment. The library also houses a museum with exhibits about Grant's personal and political life.

The library and museum are housed on the fourth floor of the Mitchell Memorial Library at Mississippi State University. The museum is open weekdays and some Saturdays during the academic year. Admission is free.

RUTHERFORD B. HAYES

OUR NINETEENTH PRESIDENT

FAST FACTS ABOUT RUTHERFORD B. HAYES

- Nineteenth president of the United States
- Born on October 4, 1822; died on January 17, 1893
- Served one term: 1877–81
- Married Lucy Webb (1831–1889) in 1852
- Children: Birchard Austin (1853–1926), Webb Cook (1856–1934), Rutherford Platt (1858–1927), Joseph Thompson (1861–1863), George Cook (1864–1866), Fanny (1867–1950), Scott Russell (1871–1923) and Manning Force (1873–1874)
- Had the first telephone in the White House
- Held the first Easter Egg Roll on the White House lawn in 1878
- Prior careers: attorney, military officer, politician

ALL ABOUT RUTHERFORD B. HAYES

Rutherford B. Hayes became our nineteenth president as the result of a controversial 1876 election that traded Electoral College votes for a promise to end Reconstruction, allowing some southern states to reinstate local governments that allowed the persecution and disenfranchisement of Black

Rutherford B. Hayes, circa
1877. *Library of Congress,*
Prints and Photographs Division.

people. This was an ironic turn of events, as Hayes considered himself a
supporter of the rights of freedmen and his early career involved defending
fugitive slaves and advocating for voting rights for all men, regardless of
color. During his four years in the White House, Hayes focused instead
on broader reform efforts: professionalizing the civil service system and
advancing public education.

EARLY LIFE

Rutherford Birchard Hayes had an inauspicious entry to the world on
October 4, 1822. The entire Hayes family had been struck down with
typhoid fever the summer before his birth, and after just three days of illness,
his father, Rutherford Hayes Jr., died at the end of July. The rest of the
family recovered from the fever but were deep in mourning, and his mother,
Sophia Birchard Hayes, was struggling to make ends meet when Rud, as he

was known, was born. The new arrival was a sickly baby and not expected to survive his first year. Although Rud defied the odds and overcame his early weak health, his family continued to be protective of him throughout his childhood.

Rud was descended from old New England stock on both sides of his family. The extended Hayes and Birchard families lived in southern Vermont, but an epidemic of spotted fever ravaged the state in 1812 and 1813, followed by a brutally cold winter in 1816. The senior Rutherford was co-owner of a country store in Dummerston, Vermont, and found that he had fewer and fewer customers. Facing dire prospects, he sold his share of the store, packed up the family and headed west to try his hand at farming on the Ohio frontier. In addition to their two young children, the Hayes family included Sophia's teenage brother, Sardis, whom she had been caring for since their mother's death several years earlier.

The Hayes family settled in Delaware, Ohio, about thirty miles north of Columbus. Delaware had a population of about four hundred people when the Hayes family moved there, including several fellow Vermont transplants. The couple purchased a 125-acre farm outside of Delaware and an unfinished house in town. The senior Rutherford worked as a farmer and ran a distillery. The family joined the local Presbyterian church. Sophia later credited Rud's survival to her strong religious faith; it also likely helped her endure continued family tragedy: in addition to her husband's death, she also lost a daughter to typhoid fever and a son to an accidental drowning.

To survive after her husband's death, Sophia rented out the farm and took in boarders to supplement the family income. Her younger brother Sardis moved out to seek his fortune elsewhere but continued to contribute financially to his sister's family and served as a surrogate father to the two surviving Hayes children, Rud and his sister, Fanny. Sardis would continue to play an important role in Rud's life, funding his education, guiding his career and even building a home for his family.

Rud attended local schools until the age of thirteen, when his uncle Sardis, by then a successful businessman in Lower Sandusky (now Fremont), Ohio, arranged for Rud to attend Norwalk Seminary in Norwalk, Ohio. Rud spent a year there and then transferred to a college preparatory school in Middletown, Connecticut. After graduation, he was admitted to Kenyon College in Gambier, Ohio. Rud was a good student, became involved in a literary and theater club and particularly enjoyed public speaking. He graduated as valedictorian in 1842 and, again with the encouragement and funding of his uncle, enrolled in Harvard Law School.

EARLY CAREER

Rutherford B. Hayes graduated from Harvard with a bachelor of laws degree in 1845 and was admitted to the Ohio bar. He lived near his uncle in Lower Sandusky for a few years and then relocated to Cincinnati, where he opened a law office. He was involved in defending a few high-profile murder cases in the early 1850s and became partner in the law firm of Corwine, Hayes and Rogers. Hayes was also an abolitionist and took pride in having defended several fugitive slaves who had escaped across the Ohio River to Cincinnati from the bordering slave state of Kentucky.

His law career well underway, Hayes met and married Lucy Ware Webb, originally from Chillicothe, Ohio, who was attending Ohio Wesleyan University in Delaware. The couple were engaged in 1851 and married the following year. Lucy Hayes was described by her contemporaries as smart and outgoing. She would become the first first lady to hold a college degree. The two welcomed a total of eight children over the next two decades; five survived to adulthood.

Lucy and Rutherford B. Hayes on their wedding day, December 30, 1852. *Library of Congress, Prints and Photographs Division.*

Hayes was initially a member of the Whig Party but migrated to the Republican Party because of his strong feelings in support of the abolition of slavery. His first venture into politics was in 1858, when he was elected city attorney in Cincinnati, stepping in after the original officeholder died. He was reelected two years later and served until April 1861, when he lost reelection and returned to his law practice.

CIVIL WAR

Rutherford B. Hayes had only just returned to his law career when shots were fired at Fort Sumter in South Carolina, signaling the beginning of what would become the Civil War. With the encouragement of his wife, Hayes enlisted in the Twenty-Third Ohio Volunteer Infantry, a group largely composed of men from northern Ohio, including another future U.S. president, William McKinley. Hayes was promoted to major and initially stationed at Camp Jackson outside Columbus, Ohio. Hayes and the Twenty-Third Ohio would spend most of the first year of the Civil War in western Virginia, guarding the railroad lines and participating in several small battles. For a brief time, Hayes made use of his law background, as he was detailed out as a judge advocate, traveling from camp to camp to provide legal advice and prosecuting any violations of military law. He was promoted to lieutenant colonel that fall and returned to the Twenty-Third Ohio.

In the summer of 1862, Hayes and the Twenty-Third Ohio participated in the Union Army of the Potomac campaign leading up to the Battle of Antietam in September; Hayes did not actually fight at Antietam, as he had been severely injured at the Battle of South Mountain near Boonsboro, Maryland, just a few days earlier. He was shot in the left arm while leading a charge. After receiving word of his injury, Lucy joined him in camp, nursing both her husband and other injured soldiers back to health before returning home to Ohio.

In October 1862, Hayes was promoted to colonel and then brevet brigadier general with command of the First Brigade, Second Kanawha Division. They spent the winter and spring at Fort Scammon (aka Camp White) near Charleston, Virginia (now West Virginia). It was there, during a visit by Lucy and their children in June 1863, that their fourth child—an eighteen-month-old son—died of dysentery. It seemed that Rud and Lucy would not be immune from the tragedy of childhood mortality that had plagued their parents' generation.

By the spring of 1864, the Second Kanawha had been reassigned to the Army of West Virginia and spent the summer and fall fighting in the Shenandoah Valley of Virginia. Hayes fought at battles in Lexington, Winchester and Cedar Creek. He was eventually promoted to brevet major general and retired from the military in June 1865—almost four years to the day after his initial enlistment.

ROAD TO THE WHITE HOUSE

While he was still serving in the Union army, the Republican Party nominated Rutherford B. Hayes to serve in the U.S. House of Representatives. Although he refused to leave military service to campaign, he was elected. Congress eventually assembled in December 1865, and Hayes joined as a moderate Republican but often voting with the Radical Republican majority on matters relating to Reconstruction in the South. Hayes was reelected to the U.S. House of Representatives in 1866 but resigned before the end of his term to run for governor of Ohio. His resignation from Congress may also have been due, in part, to a desire to return home to Ohio. A second young son had died in 1866 of scarlet fever, as had Hayes's mother, with whom he was close. Hayes was also likely pleased to be back home in time to welcome the arrival of what would be his first and only daughter, born in September 1867 and named after his beloved sister Fanny.

Hayes served two two-year terms as governor of Ohio, during which time he advocated for voting rights for freedmen and supported prison reform and state institutions for orphans and the mentally ill. He also worked to establish a state agricultural college, what would eventually become The Ohio State University.

Hayes chose not to run for a third term as governor of Ohio, instead opting to focus on his family and interests in travel, history and family genealogy. In 1873, Rud's uncle, Sardis Birchard, who never married, deeded his home in Fremont, Ohio, to his nephew. The Hayes family moved into Spiegel Grove, and Sardis, who died the following January, spent his last few months enjoying the raucous activities of his great-niece and great-nephews.

When 1875 rolled around, Hayes was nominated again as Republican candidate for governor of Ohio. He accepted, and when he won, Hayes became the first person to be elected three times to the role. His popularity within the Republican Party also made him a possible candidate for a presidential run the following year.

THE DISPUTED PRESIDENTIAL ELECTION OF 1876

In June 1876, at the Republican National Convention held in Cincinnati, Ohio, Rutherford B. Hayes was nominated as the Republican candidate for U.S. president. Samuel J. Tilden, governor of New York, was nominated as the Democratic candidate a few days later. Both candidates were viewed as honest, competent men, and both supported civil service reform and the stabilization of the economy, suffering from a post–Civil War economic depression that had worsened after the failure of a railroad investment firm in 1873. Hayes specifically campaigned on equal rights for freedmen, women's rights and the separation of powers within the federal government.

Americans went to the polls on November 7, 1876, and cast their votes for president. By that evening, it appeared that Tilden had won the popular vote by about 200,000 votes. More important, though, were the votes in the Electoral College, which would determine the president. Tilden initially had 184 electoral votes to Hayes's 165 votes—a lead, but 1 vote shy of the 185 electoral votes needed for a victory. The remaining 19 electoral votes—from Florida, Louisiana and South Carolina (plus one disputed vote from Oregon where the elector was disqualified)—were in dispute, with both Republicans and Democrats claiming wins.

The disputed election of 1876 can only be understood within the larger context of the post–Civil War reconstruction of the South. After the end of the war, former Confederate states that wanted to rejoin the United States had to, among other things, rewrite their state constitutions with certain requirements, including a statement on the abolition of slavery. Gradually, the southern states complied and were permitted to reestablish state governments and send new congressmen to Washington. But on a local level, southern governments began enacting Black Codes that placed restrictions on where and how freedmen could work and live and travel, basically forcing them back into slavery-like plantation work. Congress pushed back with the Reconstruction Act of 1867, which sent the U.S. Army into the South to force state ratifications of the Fourteenth Amendment, granting equal rights to freedmen. Even as the southern

The Electoral Commission holding a secret session to determine who would win the 1876 U.S. presidential election. *Illustration from* Frank Leslie's Illustrated Newspaper, *vol. 44, no. 119, March 10, 1877, p. 9. Library of Congress, Prints and Photographs Division.*

states ratified the amendment and Black men were finally able to both vote and get elected to political offices in the South, white supremacist groups such as the Ku Klux Klan continued with violence and intimidation to try to reverse the gains that had been made. At various times, U.S. military troops were sent into southern states to put down racial violence or support local Republican officeholders.

By the time of the 1876 presidential election, federal troops had withdrawn from all the former Confederate states except for three where they were still needed to support Republican state governments. Those three states—Florida, Louisiana and South Carolina—were the very ones where electoral votes were being contested. All three states reported voting numbers that pointed to a Tilden win, but the Republican Party argued that tens of thousands of votes were invalid because of intentionally misleading ballots, violence and voter intimidation in those states. Representatives from both parties were sent to supervise ballot recounts. By early December, the matter had still not been settled, and each party submitted electoral certificates that would result in a win for their candidate. The issue was then bumped up to Congress, where the president of the Senate would be responsible for counting the electoral votes. But what votes should he count—the ones submitted by the Republicans or the Democrats?

With the issue still not resolved by the end of January 1877, Congress established a fifteen-member electoral commission tasked with coming to a decision about who should be the next U.S. president. The commission was composed of five Republicans, five Democrats and five members of the U.S. Supreme Court. While the commission debated in public, political wrangling continued behind closed doors. Eventually, leaders from both parties reached an informal backroom agreement that came to be known as the Compromise of 1877: the Democrats would agree to the election of Hayes if he agreed to withdraw the remaining federal troops from the South, effectively ending Reconstruction and returning political control of the state governments of Florida, Louisiana and South Carolina to the Democrats. When the electoral commission finally adjourned on March 2, they had determined that all 20 disputed electoral votes would be given to Hayes. With a final electoral vote count of 185 to 184, Hayes would be the nineteenth president of the United States.

"HIS FRAUDULENCY" THE PRESIDENT

To say that not everyone agreed with the outcome of the election would be a gross understatement. Many Democrats refused to acknowledge Rutherford B. Hayes as president, referring to him as "Ruther*fraud*" and "His Fraudulency" in the press. Radical Republicans were also not happy with the compromise, accurately predicting that the withdrawal of federal troops from Florida, Louisiana and South Carolina would result in further disenfranchisement of Blacks in those states and across the rest of the Deep South.

Nevertheless, Hayes took the oath of office on March 3, 1877, and subsequently ordered the removal of the remaining federal troops from the South. Reconstruction was over. The Gilded Age, however, was just beginning.

The Gilded Age was a period of rapid industrialization, immigration and urbanization in the United States that began circa 1877 and continued until circa 1900. During this period, the United States was transformed from a primarily rural, agrarian nation into one where a majority of people lived in cities and towns. Many of those city dwellers hailed from abroad, largely from southern and eastern Europe. The immigrants found low-wage work in the numerous factories that were springing up in northern cities, in the coal

Mrs. U. S. "Thanks, Mr. TILDEN. I have promised to dance this set with Mr. HAYES."

This political cartoon, which appeared in *Harper's Weekly* on March 17, 1877, shows "Mrs. U.S." refusing Samuel Tilden in favor of President-elect Rutherford B. Hayes. *Image published with permission of ProQuest LLC. Further reproduction is prohibited without permission.*

mines of Appalachia and on the railroads being built across the West. Child labor was rampant, safety regulations were nonexistent and unions were only just beginning to exert their power. Socially, the era is best symbolized by the gap between the phenomenally wealthy industrialists (Vanderbilts, Astors, Carnegies) and the poor and young people who worked in their factories.

On the political front, the Gilded Age was a time of corrupt politics at all levels. Municipal governments were unable to keep up with the demands of their rapidly growing communities, so political machines such as New York's Tammany Hall provided the services that local individuals and businesses needed in return for votes and party loyalty. On a federal level, the political graft translated to a patronage system that gave civil service jobs to political supporters rather than those most qualified for the positions.

Hayes was one of many who hoped to eliminate the patronage system but had only limited success. After the election, Hayes refused to give seats in his cabinet to Republican loyalists, which placed him at odds with members of his own party. He also issued an executive order that said federal officeholders shouldn't engage in party politics and argued for federal funding of civil service reform, which was denied by Congress. In the end, Hayes wasn't wholly successful in his attempts at reform, but he did move the political will in that general direction, eventually leading to reform under subsequent administrations.

Also during his time in office, Hayes navigated what came to be known as the Great Railroad Strike of 1877. Following the economic downturn beginning in 1873, railroads began reducing the wages of railroad workers across the country. Things finally came to a head in July 1877, when union negotiations broke down and workers in West Virginia went on strike. The governor of West Virginia deployed state militia to intervene on the behalf of the railroads, and strikers fought back. The strike quickly spread to nearby states, and clashes between strikers and state militias turned violent. State governors from four states asked Hayes to send federal troops to support the state militias. Hayes reluctantly agreed, making 1877 the first time that federal troops were used to put down a labor strike, setting a precedent for future deployments of federal resources to protect private property— something that would continue under subsequent administrations.

The four years that the Hayes family spent in the White House were not all focused on politics. There were two children still living at home and three

Rutherford B. Hayes and family on the verandah of their home, circa 1887. *Courtesy of Hayes Presidential Library & Museums.*

others who often visited from college. A longtime teetotaler, Lucy banned the consumption of alcohol at the White House. She was still a dutiful hostess and encouraged music, informal visits and entertainment, including the first Easter egg hunt on the White House lawn in 1878.

Hayes had promised during his presidential campaign to serve for only one term, and he kept that promise. When nominations for the 1880 election rolled around, Hayes cast his support behind fellow Ohio Republican James A. Garfield. And he eagerly planned for his retirement to his Fremont home.

POST-PRESIDENCY LIFE

Rutherford B. Hayes left the White House and returned to Spiegel Grove, where he spent his retirement serving on various educational and charitable boards and traveling. He served on the board of trustees of The Ohio State University and as president of the Ohio Archaeological and Historical Society.

His wife, Lucy, died following a stroke in 1889. Rutherford died on January 17, 1893, at the age of seventy, following a heart attack. Both were buried on the grounds of their home in Fremont, Ohio.

RUTHERFORD B. HAYES HISTORIC SITES IN OHIO

Rutherford B. Hayes Birthplace
17 East William Street, Delaware, OH

The house where Rutherford B. Hayes was born is no longer standing. It had fallen into disrepair by the early 1920s, and the site was purchased by Standard Oil Company, which offered to sell it back to the community, but local organizations were unable to raise enough money. The house was torn down in 1926, and a gas station was built at the location. A historical marker now identifies the site.

Rutherford B. Hayes Presidential Library & Museum
Spiegel Grove, Fremont, OH
419-332-2081
rbhayes.org

The Rutherford B. Hayes Presidential Library & Museum is in Fremont, Ohio, and comprises the Rutherford B. Hayes Home, the Hayes Research Library and a museum telling the story of the Hayes family and presidency.

The Rutherford B. Hayes Home was built by Rutherford's uncle, Sardis Birchard, beginning in 1859. The bachelor Birchard had supported his nephew from childhood and built the house as a summer estate that he could share with the growing Hayes family. He named it Spiegel Grove in reference to the puddles of water that he noticed on the grounds that would reflect the tree branches like mirrors; *spiegel* is a German word for "mirror." The house was originally a two-story, eight-bedroom brick home. After his uncle's death, Rutherford inherited the house and over the next twenty years expanded it into an eighteen-bedroom mansion that included a library, reception room, expanded dining room, servants' rooms and indoor plumbing.

Spiegel Grove in Fremont, Ohio, was built by Sardis Birchard for his nephew, Rutherford B. Hayes, and his family. *Courtesy of Hayes Presidential Library & Museums.*

The Hayes family lived in the house from 1873 to 1875 and then returned there in 1881 for Rutherford's retirement. After his death, four additional generations lived at Spiegel Grove and offered tours of the first floor of the house beginning in the 1960s. The estate was eventually turned over to the State of Ohio and is currently operated by the Ohio History Connection.

The first floor and a portion of the second floor of the home are interpreted to the time that Rutherford and Lucy lived in the house with their children. Almost all the furnishings and other items in the home are original and in their original locations. Rutherford had professional photographs taken of the main rooms of his home, and museum curators were able to use those as reference for their restoration work. The remainder of the second floor is furnished with mid-twentieth-century family pieces. Among the notable pieces are a selection of family portraits and a portable sewing machine that Lucy took with her while visiting Rutherford at Civil War encampments. The tour also includes the house's single original bathroom, complete with running water, flush toilet and a mini library of books. (Hayes apparently used the bathroom as a place to escape from his active family.)

Twenty-five of the original acres are still part of Spiegel Grove, and there are several walking trails through the wooded estate. One trail leads to the family cemetery, which includes the tomb of Rutherford and Lucy Hayes.

Efforts to build a presidential library at Spiegel Grove were led by the second Hayes son, Webb Cook Hayes. With the financial support of the State of Ohio, they broke ground for the new building in 1912, and the Hayes Presidential Library opened in 1916. Subsequent renovations greatly added to the footprint of the building and transformed it into what is now a fifty-two-thousand-square-foot museum. The library collection was relocated into a third-floor addition and is now the Hayes Research Library.

The current museum tells the story of the life and times of Rutherford and Lucy Hayes and related historical topics. It consists of two floors of permanent exhibits about the Hayes family and Rutherford's presidency and post-presidential life. Included among the artifacts on display are Lucy's wedding dress, engagement and wedding rings and formal clothing worn by the youngest Hayes children. The museum also includes an exhibit of period weapons, a display of Fanny Hayes's dollhouses, a collection of items relating to other presidents collected by the family and two galleries of temporary exhibits.

The Hayes Research Library is located within the museum and is composed of Rutherford's twelve-thousand-volume personal library and archival material from his career. An additional eighty thousand books, periodicals and

The drawing room at the Hayes family home, Spiegel Grove, in Fremont, Ohio. *Courtesy of Hayes Presidential Library & Museums.*

other material relating to Hayes, Ohio history and genealogy have been added to the library over the past century and are available for research.

The Rutherford B. Hayes Presidential Library & Museum is open daily, with reduced hours from January to April. Admission to the grounds and the Hayes Research Library is free; a fee is charged for admission to the museum and guided tours of the Hayes Home.

Lucy Hayes Heritage Center
90 West Sixth Street, Chillicothe, OH
740-775-5829

Lucy Ware Webb, future wife of Rutherford B. Hayes, was born on August 28, 1831, in this small Federal-style house in Chillicothe, Ohio. Her father died when she was just two years old during a cholera epidemic. When Lucy was twelve years old, her mother moved the family to Delaware, Ohio, where Lucy enrolled in Ohio Wesleyan University. It was there that she met her future husband. Lucy later transferred to Cincinnati Wesleyan Female College and graduated from there in 1850.

Lucy Ware Webb, future wife of Rutherford B. Hayes, was born in this house in Chillicothe, Ohio. *Author's collection.*

The Webb house in Chillicothe was built in 1825 and was originally located on Fourth Street but was relocated in 1883 to preserve it from demolition. A group of local residents began restoration work on the house in 1968. The parlor and bedroom of the house contain period antiques, and a second bedroom contains a collection of photographs, letters, postcards and other ephemera relating to the Webb and Hayes families.

The Lucy Hayes Heritage Center is operated by a volunteer Friends of Lucy Hayes organization and is open for guided tours on Fridays and Saturdays from April through September. Admission is free, but donations are welcome.

JAMES A. GARFIELD

OUR TWENTIETH PRESIDENT

FAST FACTS ABOUT JAMES A. GARFIELD

- Twentieth president of the United States
- Born on November 19, 1831; died on September 19, 1881
- Served from March to September 1881
- Married Lucretia Rudolph (1832–1918) in 1858.
- Children: Eliza Arabella (1860–1863), Harry Augustus (1863–1942), James Rudolph (1865–1950), Mary (1867–1947), Irvin McDowell (1870–1951), Abram (1872–1958) and Edward (1874–1876)
- Previous careers: teacher, military officer, politician
- Assassinated six months after becoming president

ALL ABOUT JAMES A. GARFIELD

James A. Garfield was the last U.S. president to be born in a log cabin, and his story of overcoming early adversity through hard work and luck seems like the plot of a Horatio Algers novel. And, in fact, the mid-nineteenth-century young adult author wrote a fictionalized biography of Garfield—*From Canal Boat to President*—dedicating it in 1881 to the Garfield children, "whose

James A. Garfield, circa 1870.
*Library of Congress, Prints and
Photographs Division.*

private sorrow is the public grief." The sorrow to which Algers referred was the death of their father earlier that year, due not to an assassin's bullet but to the bungled medical attention given to the president's wounds by doctors charged with his care. Garfield was an advocate for public education and civil rights during his seventeen years in Congress; one wonders what he might have been able to accomplish as president had he not died after just six months in office.

EARLY YEARS

James A. Garfield was born in 1831 in a log cabin in what is now Moreland Hills, Ohio, about twenty miles southeast of Cleveland. He was the youngest of five children of Eliza Ballou and Abram Garfield. The Garfields were members of the Disciples of Christ, an evangelical Christian group that came into existence during the Protestant revival of the early nineteenth century and was popular on the frontier. Abram had moved to Ohio with his brother to find work on the Ohio and Erie Canal, and eventually the two brothers married sisters and purchased a piece of undeveloped land on which to build their homes and farms. When James was just a toddler, his father died of exhaustion after fighting a fire that nearly destroyed their home. His mother, Eliza, sold off much of their property to make ends meet and then continued to farm the remaining land with her young children. It was a hardscrabble life that Eliza desperately hoped for her youngest child to escape by getting a proper education. Instead, at the age of sixteen, James left home to work leading mules pulling boats along the Ohio and Erie Canal.

To Eliza's relief, her youngest son did not last long on the canals. Over the course of his first six weeks away, James nearly drowned several times and then came down with malaria. After he spent time recovering at home, his mother extracted a promise that he would take the small bit of money she had saved and go to school. James first enrolled in the Baptist-run Geauga Seminary in Chester County, Ohio, where he met his future wife, Lucretia Rudolph. James and Lucretia then attended the Western Reserve Eclectic Institute (later Hiram College) in Hiram, Ohio, which Lucretia's father had founded in 1850 with other members of the Disciples of Christ. James then transferred to Williams College in Williamstown, Massachusetts, from which he graduated as salutatorian in 1856. Throughout his studies, James worked variously as a carpenter's assistant, janitor and teacher in order to fund his education. He also preached at local churches, gaining a reputation as a capable and passionate public speaker.

Reproduction of the log cabin where James A. Garfield was born. *Photograph by Geoffrey Mendelsohn and courtesy of the Moreland Hills Historical Society.*

James A. Garfield and his family, circa 1882. *Kurz & Allison Litho. Library of Congress, Prints and Photographs Division.*

James returned to Ohio after his graduation from Williams College and took a position teaching at the Western Reserve Eclectic Institute. Lucretia had spent the past several years teaching in Cleveland, Ohio, and the two were reunited. James became head of the Eclectic Institute in 1857 at the age of twenty-six, and the following year, Lucretia and James were married. The two eventually had seven children, five of whom lived to adulthood. They set up their home in Hiram, not far from her parents' house, and James began studying law.

James was admitted to the Ohio bar and became the youngest member of the Ohio Senate when he was elected in 1859, representing northern central Ohio. He served less than two years, however, as events soon disrupted the course of Garfield's life and challenged the future of the nation.

MILITARY CAREER

When the Civil War broke out in the spring of 1861, James A. Garfield was eager to join the effort. He spent the first few months of the war recruiting soldiers throughout northeastern Ohio. In August 1861, he accepted a commission as colonel for the Forty-Second Ohio Infantry and quickly recruited his former students to fill his regiment. The Forty-Second Ohio joined the Army of the Ohio and was sent to fight Confederates in eastern Kentucky.

Garfield led just one battle during the Civil War but saw action in Kentucky, Tennessee, Mississippi and Georgia. In January 1862, he was instructed to force the Confederates out of eastern Kentucky and back into Virginia. In what would become known as the Battle of Middle Creek, Garfield divided his troops and attacked the Confederates from three sides, tricking them into believing that he had more troops than he did. The move was successful, and the Union was able to claim control of that part of the state. Garfield was promoted to brigadier general with command of the Twentieth Brigade of the Army of the Ohio, which saw action at the Battle of Shiloh in southwestern Tennessee in April.

By the summer of 1862, Garfield had taken ill and returned to Ohio to recuperate. While there, he was elected to the U.S. House of Representatives but didn't take his seat for another year. Instead, he obtained a position as chief of staff to Major General William S. Rosecrans of the Army of the Cumberland. During the Battle of Chickamauga in northwestern Georgia in September 1863, Garfield helped save the Union side from complete obliteration by calling in reinforcements after Rosecrans made some strategic mistakes. Garfield was subsequently promoted to major general, a position from which he retired in December 1863.

CONGRESSIONAL CAREER

In December 1863, James A. Garfield finally took the congressional seat to which he'd been elected in 1862. It almost did not come about, as just a few days before he was to go to Washington, his three-year-old daughter died of diphtheria. Garfield contemplated rejoining the army to distract him from his grief, but a conversation with President Abraham Lincoln persuaded him that he was needed in Congress. Garfield went on to serve a total of seventeen years in the U.S. House of Representatives, representing a district comprising the northeastern corner of Ohio, until his election to the White House in 1880.

Garfield was part of a group of Radical Republicans in Congress who believed not only in emancipation but also in the establishment of civil rights for former slaves. After Lincoln's assassination, the Radical Republicans battled with his successor, Andrew Johnson, over conflicting visions for the reunification of the nation. Congress wanted the South under military rule; Johnson granted amnesty to former Confederates. Congress passed the Civil Rights Act of 1866—granting citizenship and equal protection to former slaves—only to have it vetoed by Johnson. Congress enacted measures to restrict Johnson's ability to hire and fire staff in his administration; Johnson ignored them. Eventually, the conflict came to a head in February 1868 when Johnson fired his Republican secretary of war in violation of a newly passed act that required congressional approval for removal of appointed officials. Garfield was among the members of the Republican-led House of Representatives who retaliated by impeaching Johnson—making him the first president to be so charged; the Senate voted against conviction.

Despite the turmoil, Congress succeeded in passing two amendments to the U.S. Constitution that provided a measure of protection and support for formerly enslaved people in the United States. The Fourteenth Amendment, ratified in 1868, granted citizenship and equal protection to former slaves, and the Fifteenth Amendment, ratified in 1870, gave all men the right to vote, regardless of color or former state of enslavement. The enforcement of those protections and rights would vary greatly across the nation, but there was a time from circa 1869 to 1877 when Black political participation was on the rise. Also on the rise were attacks on Blacks across the South in the form of harassment, voter intimidation and violence—often by members of a newly formed white supremacist terrorist group: the Ku Klux Klan.

Relations between the president and Congress settled down a bit when Republican Ulysses S. Grant took office in 1869 and Garfield's role in the House of Representatives shifted toward figuring out the financial aspects of rebuilding a nation that had been decimated by Civil War. Garfield advocated for the lifting of some of the tariff restrictions that had been put in place during the war, in favor of increasing trade with other nations. He also argued that U.S. currency should continue to be backed by the gold standard and for the recalling of paper "greenbacks" that had been issued as emergency currency during the war and whose existence was contributing to inflation across the country. Garfield also had a special interest in science and natural history and helped create the U.S. Geological Survey in 1879 with a mission to study and map the landscape of the American West.

Garfield's congressional career was not without controversy, however. In the summer of 1872, news broke of his involvement in what became known as the Crédit Mobilier affair: a scam where a fake company was set up to

Statue of James A. Garfield at Hiram College in Hiram, Ohio. *Author's collection.*

take federal money that was supposed to fund railroad construction and was instead diverted into stock that was offered to congressmen as bribes. Garfield had accepted stock but claimed ignorance of the scheme. In 1873, Garfield was chair of the appropriations committee when Congress voted themselves a 50 percent raise—a move that was widely criticized. And in the spring of 1874, Garfield—who was still working as a part-time lawyer to supplement his congressional salary—received an unusually large payment to represent a contractor who was bidding on a Washington public works project. The press found out and criticized Garfield for what was, at best, a conflict of interest and, at worst, payment for his political connections.

Despite the controversy, by 1880, Garfield was nearly twenty years into his political career and was a respected and sought-after member of the Republican leadership. In January, he was selected to serve in the Senate to represent Ohio, a sign of his status in the party. Garfield had not yet expressed any presidential ambition, but everything would change over the course of seven days in early June 1880 at the Republican National Convention in Chicago, Illinois.

ROAD TO THE WHITE HOUSE

There were three presumed candidates leading up to the 1880 Republican National Convention: Ulysses S. Grant, who had already served two terms as president and spent the ensuing years on an around-the-world tour with his wife; Senator James G. Blaine of Maine, who had previously served as Speaker of the House; and Senator John Sherman of Ohio, who had served as secretary of the treasury with responsibility for the development of the national banking system. The current president, Republican Rutherford B. Hayes, had announced that he had no interest in a second term in office. Delegates from across the nation gathered in Chicago to begin debate and voting.

James A. Garfield had been recruited to give the nomination speech for Sherman, a fellow Ohioan, and delivered it on June 5. Depending on the reports, his speech was either so powerful that delegates began discussing Garfield as a nominee or it was only mediocre because Garfield had planned all along to present himself as a dark horse candidate for the nomination. Either way, when balloting began a few days later, none of the three official nominees had a clear lead. Over the course of the next two days, delegates' votes gradually shifted toward Garfield. Finally, after thirty-six rounds of ballots—and over his objections that may or may not have been for show—Garfield was selected as the Republican Party's nominee for the presidency.

Despite his initial reluctance, Garfield accepted the candidacy and resigned from his Senate seat. During this period, it was still viewed as undignified for a

Broadside showing James A. Garfield and Chester A. Arthur, circa 1880. *Vic Arnold and A.S. Seer's Lith & Print. Library of Congress, Prints and Photographs Division.*

presidential candidate to stump for his own campaign, so Garfield spent most of the next several months at home in Mentor, Ohio. However, the people came to him. Garfield found himself spending hours and days greeting visitors and giving speeches from his home, in what came to be known as a "front porch campaign"—the first of its kind. In the end, he was successful, beating Democratic nominee Winfield Scott Hancock of Pennsylvania and earning himself a seat as the twentieth president of the United States.

Garfield spent the months leading up to his inauguration selecting his cabinet; his wife persuaded Congress to appropriate $30,000 for the renovation and redecorating of the White House. The Garfield family—including five children and their grandmother—moved into the executive mansion in March 1881. Garfield began planning his priorities for the year, including rooting out corrupt high-level employees within the U.S. Post Office Department and revisiting his attempts at introducing federal government-funded universal education. He was also interested in expanding international trade and increasing American influence over the Kingdom of Hawaii as a strategic location for trade with Asia. Little did anyone know that Garfield would not have the time to follow through on any of his aspirations in the short time that he would serve as president.

ASSASSINATION AND LEGACY

Despite efforts by James A. Garfield and others to reform the patronage-based civil service system, in 1880, it was still generally expected that a newly elected president would appoint his political supporters and friends to government jobs as a thank-you for their loyalty during the election campaign. It was also accepted that supporters and job seekers could show up at the White House and plead their cases. Literally hundreds of people milled through the public rooms of the executive mansion and federal offices in hopes of catching a word with the president during his daily public calling hours.

One of the people who became an uninvited regular at the White House following Garfield's election was a ne'er-do-well named Charles J. Guiteau. Guiteau had a troubled history involving time in a religious cult, a failed law career and a history of petty crime and theft. During the 1880 presidential campaign, Guiteau had developed an interest in politics. He wrote a speech in support of Garfield that he mailed to prominent Republicans and may have delivered to a small audience once or twice. Guiteau believed that he was owed a high-level political appointment for what he believed was his contribution to Garfield's success—he expressed preference for a consulship to Paris or Vienna.

There was, of course, no chance of Guiteau obtaining any sort of position in the Garfield administration, and he was eventually told as much. But Guiteau still spent hours writing letters pleading his case and days sitting in the White House waiting room. As he was rebuked more and more often by staffers, Guiteau gradually came to believe that Garfield was a liability to the Republican Party and that Chester A. Arthur, Garfield's vice president, would be a better executive. At some point in the spring of 1881, Guiteau began to formulate a plan to assassinate the president.

After the fact, Guiteau happily confessed his plan and the steps he took to carry it out. He borrowed fifteen dollars to purchase a gun and visited the jail where he was likely to be taken to assess the quality of the facilities. He spent several weeks stalking Garfield and came close to shooting him at least two times—including once while the president was attending church with his family. On the day of the assassination, Guiteau placed a letter in his shirt pocket with a statement saying that the president's death was necessary to unite the nation and made his way to the Baltimore and Potomac Railroad Station on the corner of B and 6th Streets NW in Washington, D.C.

Scene of the assassination of James A. Garfield, 1881. *Library of Congress, Prints and Photographs Division.*

On July 2, 1881, Garfield was awaiting a train to Massachusetts to embark on his summer vacation when he was approached from the rear by Guiteau. Guiteau pulled his gun and fired twice, grazing Garfield in the arm and hitting him squarely in the back. Garfield collapsed to the ground, and Guiteau was immediately arrested. If things had gone differently in the next few hours, Garfield likely would have survived his wounds. An autopsy eventually revealed that the bullet had missed all of his major organs and lodged in fatty tissue behind his pancreas. If Garfield had been simply left alone for his body to heal naturally, he would likely have joined the cadre of Civil War veterans walking the streets with slugs lodged in their bodies. But instead, Garfield fell victim to overenthusiastic doctors whose poking and prodding with unsanitary fingers and tools led to infections that would literally rot the president from the inside out.

At the time of Garfield's shooting, the profession of medicine was at a moment of transition. Well-educated physicians in the 1880s knew about what was then called "germ theory"—the now-proven theory that microscopic organisms cause disease—and were familiar with the work of British surgeon Joseph Lister advocating the use of carbolic acid to disinfect wounds and prevent infection. It's just that not all physicians—including the one who took the lead on treating Garfield—were well educated. There were not yet state or federal standards on medical education, and just about anyone could hang a shingle and call themselves a physician.

In the moments and hours after the shooting, several doctors probed Garfield's wounds with unsanitary fingers and tools in an attempt to locate the path of the bullet through his body. After they returned him to the White House, they continued to poke at Garfield's injury, introducing germs that ravaged through his body. They also treated him with large doses of morphine and other drugs that caused stomach upset and vomiting, eventually adding malnutrition to the list of the president's ailments. Garfield dropped from 225 to 130 pounds and was in near-constant pain.

Offers of help poured into the White House. One of them was from Alexander Graham Bell—inventor of the telephone—who had developed a metal-detecting device that he thought might be able to locate the offending bullet. Bell tried his metal detector on Garfield twice, but the results were inconclusive—likely because he was looking for the bullet on the wrong side of the president's body. Another group, led by former explorer John Wesley Powell, assembled the country's first rudimentary air conditioning system to cool the president's bedroom. It was composed of fans, large blocks of ice and cheesecloth screens and was able to lower the temperature of the room to seventy-five degrees.

Eventually, it became clear that the president was not getting better. By early September, Garfield insisted that he be removed from Washington. Plans were made to move him to a house on the New Jersey shore to take advantage of the seaside air. He spent the last two weeks of his life in Elberton, New Jersey, with his wife and doctors. Garfield died on September 19, 1881.

An autopsy was performed immediately after Garfield's death and confirmed that the bullet had done no real damage; he died from infection. Sections of Garfield's body and brain were removed to use as evidence at Guiteau's trial and eventually made their way to the National Museum of Health and Medicine, where they still reside.

Guiteau went to trial for the president's murder in 1882. His lawyers pleaded the insanity defense on his behalf. Guiteau insisted that he had shot the president but that it was the doctors who killed him. Guiteau was found guilty and hanged on June 30, 1882.

JAMES A. GARFIELD HISTORIC SITES IN OHIO

James A. Garfield Birthplace

4350 Som Center Road, Moreland Hills, OH
440-248-1188
mhhsohio.org

James A. Garfield was born in 1831 in a log cabin on what was then the frontier of northeastern Ohio. His parents both came from the East and, after they married, purchased a piece of undeveloped land in the newly established Orange Township that they cleared for a home and farm. James, the youngest child, was just two years old when his father died. His mother raised James and his four siblings to adulthood on this farm.

Nothing remains of the original log cabin in which Garfield was born. The original birth site has been identified with a plaque, and the Moreland Hills Historical Society built a replica 1830s cabin nearby. The site is adjacent to the Moreland Hills municipal offices, and from the municipal parking lot, visitors can follow a short brick path to the replica cabin and a statue of Garfield as a boy. From there, visitors can follow a further quarter-mile trail to the original birth site.

The James A. Garfield Birthplace is free and open to the public. The replica cabin is open on Saturdays from June to September or by appointment at other times.

Hiram College

11715 Garfield Road, Hiram, OH
800-362-5280
hiram.edu/about-hiram-college/history-of-the-college/garfield-trail/

In 1850, the Disciples of Christ founded a coeducational preparatory school in rural Hiram, Ohio. One of the founders was Zebulon Rudolph, father of Lucretia Rudolph, future wife of James A. Garfield. Both James and Lucretia attended the Western Reserve Eclectic Institute in its first years, studying Greek, Latin, mathematics and geology. After finishing college in Massachusetts, James returned to teach at the institute. He was promoted to principal and worked there until the Civil War. He then filled the ranks of his regiment with institute students and alum. In 1867, the institute was renamed Hiram College.

Several buildings at Hiram College have connections to Garfield: Buckingham Place, a home on the edge of campus, was built circa 1852, and it is believed that James worked as a carpenter on the house while he was a student at the Eclectic Institute. The 1853 Garfield Robbins Zimmerman Home, located on campus, was owned by the Garfields from 1863 to 1874, and they lived in the house off and on while James served in Congress. Koritansky Hall, now classroom space, was previously a church in Mecca, Ohio, where James preached while on breaks from school; it was dismantled and moved to Hiram campus. And across the street from Koritansky Hall is another place where James is believed to have preached: the still-active Hiram Christian Church.

None of the buildings at Hiram College is open to the public, but they can be easily viewed from the sidewalk.

James A. Garfield National Historic Site

8095 Mentor Avenue, Mentor, OH
440-255-8722
nps.gov/jaga

In 1876, while serving in the U.S. House of Representatives, James A. Garfield purchased a run-down farm northeast of Cleveland in the rural community of Mentor, Ohio. He wanted his young sons—ranging in age from two to eleven years old—to learn how to farm and work with their hands, as he had when a child. By 1880, the Garfields had renovated the property's original 1832 nine-room farmhouse into a twenty-room, two-and-a-half-story home with room for James, Lucretia, their five surviving children and two grandparents. The 118-acre property also comprised a working farm, a fruit orchard and a barn with horses and other animals.

The Garfields' quiet farm life came to a rather abrupt end when James accepted the Republican Party nomination for president in the summer of 1880. For the next several months, hordes of visitors took the train to Mentor to meet the nominee and hear him speak. The Garfields converted a small building on the property into a campaign office, and James addressed visitors from the expansive front porch of his home, which reporters nicknamed "Lawnfield"—in part because visitors would sometimes camp out on the lawn while waiting for an audience with the candidate. An estimated seventeen thousand people came to Mentor (population five hundred residents) to see Garfield.

Home of James A. Garfield and his family in Mentor, Ohio. *Author's collection.*

After her husband's assassination, Lucretia returned to Mentor with their children. She used thousands of dollars in donations that had been raised by supporters to expand their home to include a memorial library, which she filled with nearly two thousand of James's books and a fireproof vault in which to store his papers. She also arranged for the construction of several outbuildings that remain today, including a windmill and a storage barn for natural gas, which was discovered on the property.

Lucretia died in 1918, and the property passed on to her children, who gradually sold off portions of the farm and then donated the house, contents and remaining land to the Western Reserve Historical Society in 1936. They ran the museum for the next four decades. The James A. Garfield National Historic Site was created by Congress in 1980, and the management of the property was gradually transferred to the National Park Service, which currently runs the site.

The site is composed of a visitor center with a small museum about Garfield's military and political career and a twenty-minute film about Garfield's life. The house is accessible via a forty-five-minute guided tour, which includes the 1880 portion of the house as well as Lucretia's 1885 addition. Most of the rooms are furnished with Garfield family furniture and decorative items. The 1885 addition comprises additional bedrooms as well as a memorial library—the first presidential library in the United States—and a fireproof vault, which contains a preserved wreath from James's funeral. The house is also notable for its original woodwork, stained-glass windows and other decorative elements.

Admission to the museum and house tours are free. The site is open daily May through October; hours are limited the rest of the year.

James A. Garfield Memorial
Lake View Cemetery
12316 Euclid Avenue, Cleveland, OH
216-421-2665
lakeviewcemetery.com/visit/garfield-memorial

After his death, James A. Garfield's body lay in state in Washington and then was transported by train back to Ohio. It was temporarily interred in Lake View Cemetery in Cleveland while an appropriate monument was constructed. A local committee raised $125,000 and held an international competition for the design of the memorial. It took nine years before the memorial was complete.

James A. Garfield Memorial in Lake View Cemetery, Cleveland, Ohio, 1890. *Library of Congress, Prints and Photographs Division.*

The James A. Garfield Memorial at Lake View Cemetery in Cleveland, Ohio, was dedicated on Memorial Day 1890. The memorial is a fifty-foot-diameter circular tower with terra-cotta panels depicting scenes from Garfield's life. Inside the tower are stained-glass windows, a mosaic dome and a statue of Garfield. A stairway leads to a balcony with a sweeping view of Cleveland and Lake Erie. Both James and Lucretia, as well as one of their daughters, are entombed there.

The memorial is free and open during the summer.

BENJAMIN HARRISON

OUR TWENTY-THIRD PRESIDENT

FAST FACTS ABOUT BENJAMIN HARRISON

- Twenty-third president of the United States
- Born on August 20, 1833; died on March 13, 1901
- Served for one term: 1889–93
- Married Caroline Scott (1832–1892) in 1853; married Mary Dimmick (1858–1948) in 1896
- Children with Caroline: Russell Benjamin (1854–1936) and Mary Scott (1858–1930); with Mary: Elizabeth (1897–1955)
- Grandfather was the ninth president (William Henry Harrison)
- First president to have electricity in the White House
- Prior careers: lawyer, military officer, politician

ALL ABOUT BENJAMIN HARRISON

Benjamin Harrison was descended from a long line of Virginia and Ohio politicians and seemed destined for a life of public service. Although born and raised in Ohio, as a young man he moved to Indianapolis and built his family and law career there. Harrison served in the Civil War, represented Indiana in the U.S. Senate for six years and was elected president in 1888,

Benjamin Harrison, 1888.
Photograph by George Prince. Library of Congress, Prints and Photographs Division.

despite losing the popular vote. His one term in office is best remembered for implementation of protective tariffs, the beginnings of anti-trust legislation and the addition of six western states to the Union.

EARLY LIFE

Benjamin Harrison was born on August 20, 1833, into a family that had been involved in U.S. politics from the very beginning. One great-grandfather, Benjamin Harrison, was a signer of the Declaration of Independence. Another great-grandfather, John Cleves Symmes, was a delegate to the Continental Congress. His grandfather William Henry Harrison was elected the ninth president of the United States when Benjamin was seven years old. His father, John Scott Harrison, served in the U.S. House of Representatives. It seemed that young Benjamin was destined for a political life.

Benjamin grew up in North Bend, Ohio, about fifteen miles west of Cincinnati at the confluence of the Miami and Ohio Rivers. Home was on a six-hundred-acre corn, wheat and hay farm known as The Point that had been carved out of his grandfather's plantation. Benjamin was an active child who loved fishing and hunting and other outdoor pursuits. He was surrounded by siblings: two from his father's first marriage and eventually five siblings from his parents' union. (An additional four siblings died as infants.) Benjamin's mother, Elizabeth Ramsey Irwin Harrison, was a devout Presbyterian, and the children were expected to participate in daily prayers and Bible readings; religion would continue to play a large role in Benjamin's life as an adult.

The Harrison family also valued education. They lived too far away to attend the village school, so Benjamin's father built a one-room schoolhouse on the plantation for his children to be tutored at home. At age fourteen, Benjamin left home to continue his education at Farmer's College, a preparatory school near Cincinnati. From there, he enrolled in Miami University in Oxford, Ohio. He was a successful student and active in the Union Literary Society. It was also in Oxford where he met the woman who would eventually become his wife, Caroline Scott.

Caroline Lavinia Scott was born and raised in Oxford, Ohio. Caroline's father was a Presbyterian minister and president of Oxford Female Institute. The couple met while Caroline was studying at the institute and Benjamin was attending the nearby university. Both graduated from their respective schools in 1852, and the couple was married the following fall.

EARLY CAREER

After graduating from Miami University, Benjamin Harrison moved to Cincinnati to study law under a local attorney. This was the time when independent study of law was still a more common path to a law career than attending law school. Harrison was admitted to the Ohio bar in 1854. Shortly thereafter, the Harrisons relocated to Indianapolis, Indiana, believing that there were better career prospects in a larger city. Benjamin also likely wanted to get out from under the shadow of his family in Ohio and strike out on his own.

In addition to an active law career, Harrison also dipped his toes in the world of politics during his time in Indianapolis. He was elected Indianapolis city attorney and took on a side gig as reporter of the Indiana state supreme court, managing the compilation and publication of the court's

Benjamin Harrison's house in Indianapolis, Indiana. *Historic American Buildings Survey. Library of Congress, Prints and Photographs Division.*

official documents. He was an active member of the Republican Party and campaigned for Abraham Lincoln in the pivotal election of 1860.

During their time in Indianapolis, the Harrisons' life centered on church and family. They had two children and were active in a local Presbyterian church where Benjamin taught Sunday school. He was also a founding member of the University Club, a private social club.

CIVIL WAR

Like thousands of other Americans, the Harrison family found their lives transformed in the spring of 1861 by the outbreak of the Civil War. Unlike many of his peers, however, Benjamin did not immediately enlist. Caroline was pregnant, and the couple was also supporting one of Benjamin's younger brothers and a nephew, so the family decided that he was needed at home. A year later, in the summer of 1862, President Abraham Lincoln sent out word that additional troops were needed in the war effort. This time, Harrison heeded the call. He recruited a regiment from throughout northern Indiana and was commissioned in as second lieutenant for the Seventieth Indiana Volunteer Regiment. Shortly after, he was promoted to captain.

General Benjamin Harrison at the Battle of Resaca, May 1864. *Kurtz & Allison. Library of Congress, Prints and Photographs Division.*

The Seventieth Indiana spent the bulk of 1862 and 1863 on garrison and guard duty in Kentucky and Tennessee. Harrison was promoted to colonel and spent the time drilling and laying down discipline on his troops. He also enacted a policy against drinking alcohol, which was likely only moderately successful, and earned a reputation as a strong leader.

In early 1864, the Seventieth Indiana joined General William Tecumseh Sherman's Army of the Cumberland in its campaign to take Atlanta. Harrison was promoted to brigade commander and participated in several battles in Georgia. At the Battle of Resaca in northwestern Georgia, Sherman's troops battled the Confederate Army of Tennessee led by Joseph E. Johnston in an attempt to cut off Confederate access to the Western and Atlantic Railroad. Harrison was recognized for successfully leading his ground troops against the Confederate artillery battery in what was otherwise an inconclusive battle. The Confederate and Union troops, including Harrison's brigade, continued to spar as Sherman advanced his troops toward Atlanta. In July, the Confederate Army of Tennessee, newly led by John Bell Hood, attacked Sherman's Union army in an attempt to stop them from crossing Peachtree Creek, north of Atlanta. They were not successful. After the battle, Harrison wrote of running out of ammunition and having to cut cartridge boxes from the bodies of Confederate soldiers to distribute to his troops.

Harrison remained with Sherman through the defeat of Atlanta but did not participate in Sherman's March to the Sea. Instead, in the fall of 1864, Harrison briefly returned to Indiana to campaign in support of Lincoln's second term, contracted scarlet fever and then was reassigned to command a brigade under Major General George H. Thomas's Army of the Cumberland in the Battle of Nashville in December 1864. Harrison ended up not returning to rejoin the Seventieth Indiana until after Confederate general Robert E. Lee surrendered to Union general Ulysses S. Grant at Appomattox Court House, Virginia, in April 1865, effectively bringing the Civil War to an end. Harrison ended his military career as brevet brigadier general two months later.

POST–CIVIL WAR CAREER

After the war, Benjamin Harrison returned to Indianapolis, his family and his law career. In 1874, the Harrisons began construction of a new home on North Delaware Street in Indianapolis. The three-story, red brick Italianate-style house would eventually have sixteen rooms, running water and gas lights—still a luxury at the time. The Harrisons lived there for the remainder of their lives.

In addition to his law career, Harrison also reengaged and deepened his involvement in Republican politics. He enjoyed public speaking and campaigned for other Republican candidates. Harrison ran for governor of Indiana in 1876 and U.S. senator in 1877, losing both times but building a reputation in state politics. In 1880, he chaired the Indiana delegation to the Republican National Convention, helping Ohioan James A. Garfield secure his nomination for president.

Later that year, Harrison was selected by the Indiana state legislature to serve in the U.S. Senate. (U.S. senators were selected by the state legislatures until the Seventeenth Amendment was passed in 1913.) He served for six years. During his time in the Senate, Harrison advocated for federal spending on pensions for Union war veterans and public education. He believed in protective tariffs to protect U.S. commerce and was a supporter of the conservation of land in the western United States. He broke from the Republican Party in opposing the Chinese Exclusion Act of 1882, which banned immigration of Chinese laborers, arguing that it jeopardized the United States' relationship with China. In 1887, Harrison lost his bid for reelection to the U.S. Senate to the Democratic candidate, likely because of gerrymandering of the legislative districts. Harrison returned to Indianapolis and, a year later, announced that he would be running for president.

The Republican National Convention met in Chicago in the summer of 1888 and nominated Harrison for U.S. president on the eighth ballot. New York banker Levi P. Marton was nominated as his running mate. His Democratic opponent was President Grover Cleveland, seeking a second term in office. Harrison borrowed the "front porch campaign" strategy that had been so successful for former president James Garfield and delivered speeches only to carefully screened supporters who traveled to his Indianapolis home. More than 300,000 people found their way to Indianapolis over the next several months, eventually forcing the candidate to relocate to a nearby public park to accommodate the crowds. The major issues in the presidential race continued to center on the same issues that Harrison advocated for while senator: protective tariffs, Civil War pensions and civil service reform.

The 1888 U.S. presidential election had a remarkable 79 percent of eligible voters cast their ballots. Harrison won the Electoral College with 233 votes to Cleveland's 168 but lost the popular vote by 90,000 votes. The Democratic Party did not contest Harrison's win, likely due to the widespread

Presidential campaign ball. The expression "get the ball rolling" came from a publicity stunt during William Henry Harrison's presidential campaign in 1840, re-created for his grandson's campaign in 1888. *Published by William B. Holmes. Library of Congress, Prints and Photographs Division.*

understanding that many southern Black Republicans had been prevented from casting their votes—which would likely have been for Harrison—due to restrictive Black Codes that had been imposed at the end of Reconstruction. Harrison was inaugurated the following March. During his speech, Harrison spoke of the importance of education, commercial growth and statehood for the territories and reaffirmed the Monroe Doctrine, which opposed any colonization in the Americas.

PRESIDENT

Benjamin Harrison's one-term presidency is often recognized for his support of African American rights and his efforts to expand the United States' role in international commerce. He was a firm supporter of the Fifteenth Amendment, which gave Black men the right to vote, and supported two bills to protect civil rights. Like his predecessors, Harrison also attempted to professionalize the civil service system and argued for hiring government employees based on their experience and skills rather than as a thank-you for political support. However, he was never completely successful in eliminating the spoils system, and it only resulted in him alienating himself from many in the Republican Party who expected their support of the president to be rewarded with a job in his administration.

Harrison was unflagging in his support for his fellow Civil War veterans. He spent an unprecedented amount of money when he signed into law the 1890 Dependent Pension Act. This granted $12 per month (about $400 per month in 2023 dollars) to disabled Union soldiers. Within four years, the U.S. government would have 37 percent of its budget set aside for pension payments.

To fund such efforts and protect U.S. business interests, Harrison believed strongly in the need for protective tariffs. These were taxes placed on the import of foreign goods to encourage the purchase of U.S.-made or -grown goods. While in the White House, Harrison supported Republican representative (and future U.S. president) William McKinley's Tariff Act of 1890, which increased duties on imports almost 50 percent, while removing tariffs on some staple goods such as sugar, tea and coffee and giving American producers federal subsidies. While intended to protect American manufacturers, the taxes resulted in higher prices for average consumers and eventually lost Harrison voter support when he was up for reelection.

The Red Room of the White House in Washington, D.C. The portrait on the right is of Caroline Harrison, circa 1890. *Photograph by Frances Benjamin Johnston. Library of Congress, Prints and Photographs Division.*

While supportive of U.S. businesses over foreign entities, Harrison also acted to limit large U.S. corporations when they threatened to create a monopoly. These efforts were the beginning of what would come to be known as the Progressive Era—a period in U.S. history when reformers attempted to mitigate the worst of the Gilded Age excesses through political and social reforms. Harrison supported the Sherman Anti-Trust Act, which sought to prevent companies from artificially inflating prices by restricting fair trade and allowed the Department of Justice and individuals to bring lawsuits against companies suspected of doing so. Harrison signed this act, the first to regulate large corporations, into law in 1890.

Harrison's presidency also saw the closing of the American frontier. After 1890, the U.S. Census Bureau reported that there were no remaining western lands that had not yet been populated by white settlers. The American frontier had held a great deal of symbolism in the nineteenth-century idea of Manifest Destiny—the belief that the United States had a

God-given responsibility to "conquer the West" and expand the nation to the Pacific Ocean. The frontier also played an important role in the legends and folklore of the Wild West and was seen by some as key to the American character. With the closing of the American frontier, some began looking to international expansion as the next frontier.

Meanwhile, little consideration was given to the original inhabitants in the conversations about the frontier. Native American tribes, which had been forced onto smaller and smaller reservation lands and forced to assimilate into western culture, now saw even those reservations opened to white encroachment. There was a movement to fight back against the white settlement, part of which resulted in the massacre of nearly three hundred Lakota by the U.S. Army in December 1890 at the Battle of Wounded Knee. Between 1889 and 1892, nearly fifteen million acres of land that had been protected for Native American tribes were opened for white settlement, over the objection of those who lived there.

By the time Harrison left office, the northwestern quadrant of the United States—the remains of the Louisiana Purchase—had been neatly divided into states. In just a two-year period, six new states were added to the Union: Montana, North Dakota, South Dakota and Washington in 1889 and Idaho and Wyoming in 1890. These new states shifted the focus of U.S. infrastructure-building to the west for several years as the new states demanded transportation, communication and water. The creation of these states also added new U.S. senators and representatives to Congress—mostly Republicans.

During his time in office, Harrison also oversaw the 1891 Land Revision Act, which impowered the president to set aside land for public use. This permitted the creation of the first federal forest on land bordering Yellowstone National Park and provided the first federal protection of a prehistoric Native American site in Casa Grande, Arizona.

In the arena of foreign affairs, Harrison attempted to expand the role of the United States. In October 1889, he convened the first Pan-American Conference. He negotiated several trade agreements, enlarged the U.S. Navy, discussed the possibility of building a canal through Central America and battled with British Canada over seal hunting in the Bering Sea. He attempted to annex Hawaii, but the Senate refused to support him, and the annexation wouldn't happen until McKinley's presidency several years later. In the spring of 1891, Harrison embarked on a cross-country speaking tour, the first time a sitting president was able to do that since the end of the Civil War.

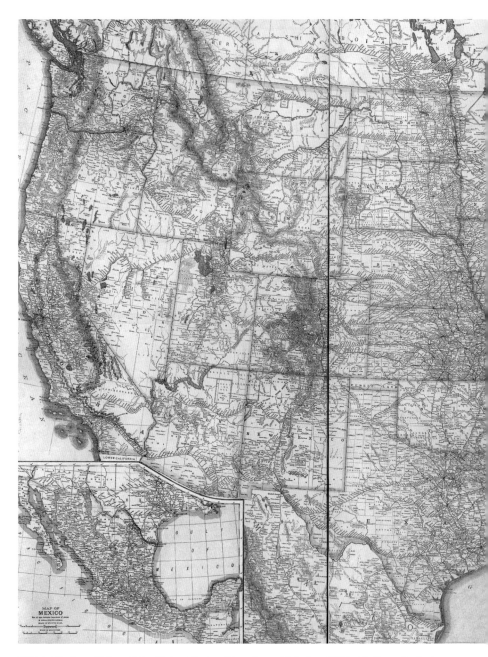

Official Railroad Map of the United States, Canada and Mexico, 1890. *Matthews-Northrup Company. Library of Congress, Geography and Map Division.*

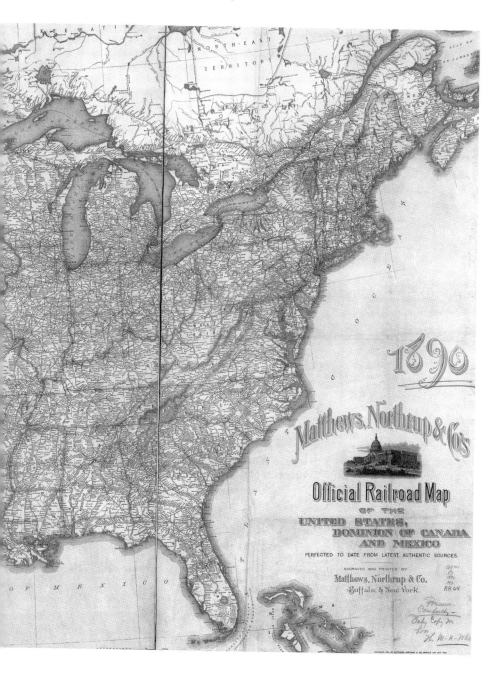

On the homefront, the White House under Harrison was a lively place. When they moved in, the Harrisons brought along their adult daughter and her family, their grown son and his family and Caroline's father. During their time in the White House, Caroline lobbied Congress for funding to renovate the nearly one-hundred-year-old building, which had fallen into disrepair. They did not fully fund her plans but did approve about $35,000, which was used to add bathrooms and modernize some of the service spaces. Congress also paid to install electricity in the White House. Caroline enjoyed entertaining and had the first Christmas tree at the White House.

Harrison was nominated for a second presidential term but only had lukewarm support from his fellow Republicans. The Democratic Party nominated former president Grover Cleveland. This was the first time in U.S. history that two former presidents were running against each other for another term. In 1892, Harrison's campaign was not as robust as four years prior, largely due to his focus being on family matters. Caroline, who suffered ongoing respiratory problems, became increasingly ill and was diagnosed with tuberculosis in September 1892. She died the following month, just two weeks before the presidential election. In the end, Cleveland won the 1892 presidential election with nearly double the number of Electoral College votes as Harrison.

POST-PRESIDENCY LIFE

In 1893, Benjamin Harrison left Washington and returned to his law practice in Indiana. He served on the board of trustees of Purdue University and wrote articles on the federal government for popular readership.

In April 1896, at the age of sixty-two, Harrison remarried. His spouse was Mary Scott Lord Dimmick, the widowed niece of his late wife, Caroline. Benjamin and Mary had a longtime and close friendship despite her being twenty-five years his junior. Mary was born in Pennsylvania and grew up in Illinois and New Jersey, where she attended private schools. She had married her first husband, Walter Dimmick, in 1881, but he died suddenly just six weeks after their wedding. During the Harrisons' time in the White House, Mary had spent lots of time with them, including serving as Caroline's secretary.

Harrison's grown children did not approve of the couple and did not attend their wedding. They remained estranged for the rest of Benjamin's life.

Cartoon depiction of Benjamin Harrison and his second wife, Mary Scott Dimmock, 1896. *Drawn by George Yost Coffin. Library of Congress, Prints and Photographs Division.*

In March 1901, Harrison came down with an illness that progressed to pneumonia. He died on March 13, 1901, at the age of sixty-seven at his home in Indianapolis, Indiana.

BENJAMIN HARRISON HISTORIC SITES IN OHIO

Benjamin Harrison Birthplace
Symmes and Washington Avenues, North Bend, OH

Benjamin Harrison was born on his family's estate in the small town of North Bend, Ohio. The house where he was born is no longer standing; a historical marker identifies the site.

William Henry Harrison Tomb Historic Site
41 Cliff Road, North Bend, OH
844-288-7709
ohiohistory.org/visit/browse-historical-sites/william-henry-harrison-tomb

Benjamin Harrison's grandfather and ninth president of the United States, William Henry Harrison, was buried on the Harrison family's estate in North Bend, Ohio. When the estate was sold, the burial ground passed to

The tomb of William Henry Harrison, ninth president of the United States and grandfather of Benjamin Harrison, in North Bend, Ohio. *Photograph by Nick Cole.*

the State of Ohio. The elder Harrison is buried here, along with his son (Benjamin Harrison's father) and other members of the family. The site is free and open daily.

Harrison-Symmes Memorial Museum
112 South Miami Avenue, Cleves, OH
hsmfmuseum.org

This small museum interprets the life of the two Harrison presidents and members of their extended family. The museum is volunteer-run and open only by appointment, which can be requested on their website. Admission is free, but donations are welcome.

BENJAMIN HARRISON HISTORIC SITES OUTSIDE OF OHIO

Benjamin Harrison Presidential Site
1230 North Delaware Street, Indianapolis, IN
317-631-1888
bhpsite.org

Benjamin Harrison purchased a plot of land in May 1868 and six years later began construction of what would become a three-story, sixteen-room Italianate-style home. Excepting the time when he was in Washington, Benjamin lived here for the rest of his life. After his death, his second wife and daughter lived in the home for a few years and then moved to New York. The house was rented out and then used as a boardinghouse and dormitory. It was first opened for tours in 1951 and underwent a comprehensive restoration in the early 2000s. The house is currently open by guided tour and features furnishings and other items that belonged to the Harrisons. There are rotating exhibits on the third-floor ballroom and the welcome center. The Benjamin Harrison Presidential Site is open daily, but hours vary. Admission is charged.

Benjamin Harrison's monument in Crown Hill Cemetery, Indianapolis, Indiana, circa 1900–10. *Detroit Publishing Company. Library of Congress, Prints and Photographs Division.*

Benjamin Harrison Grave

Crown Hill Cemetery
700 West 38th Street, Indianapolis, IN
317-920-4165
crownhillhf.org/notable/president-benjamin-harrison/

Benjamin Harrison is buried in Crown Hill Cemetery in Indianapolis, Indiana.

WILLIAM McKINLEY

OUR TWENTY-FIFTH PRESIDENT

FAST FACTS ABOUT WILLIAM McKINLEY

- Twenty-fifth president of the United States
- Born on January 29, 1843; died on September 14, 1901
- Served one term and a few months: 1897–1901
- Married Ida Saxton (1847–1907) in 1871
- Children: Katherine (1871–1875) and Ida (1873–1873)
- Was assassinated six months into his second term
- Prior careers: teacher, military officer, lawyer, politician

ALL ABOUT WILLIAM McKINLEY

William McKinley was the last president to have fought in the Civil War. During his first term in office, he led the United States to victory in the Spanish-American War and the annexation of several island nations. His focus on raising tariffs helped protect American industry at the end of the nineteenth century. His time in office was not tainted by the controversies that plagued some of his fellow Ohio presidents, and it is reasonable to believe that he would have had a successful second term, had he not been assassinated just six months later. Yet when considering McKinley, what

Left: William McKinley, circa 1900. *Library of Congress, Prints and Photographs Division.*

Opposite: Reproduction of the birthplace of William McKinley in Niles, Ohio. *Author's collection.*

stands out most are not his political accomplishments but his profound and unyielding support and nurturing of his wife, Ida, through her lifelong physical and mental illnesses.

EARLY LIFE

William McKinley was born on January 29, 1843, in the tiny mill town of Niles, Ohio, population about three hundred residents. His parents—Nancy Campbell Allison McKinley and William McKinley—came from Scotch-Irish and English ancestry and moved to Niles sometime in the 1830s. They rented a small wood frame house on the main street in Niles, and the senior William ran a blast furnace that produced raw iron to be used in steel production. It was a small-town life that revolved around church and community.

The future president was the seventh of nine children born to the McKinley family; all but one of his siblings survived to adulthood. As a young child, William attended a one-room schoolhouse just down the road from

his home and was reportedly a bright student. The McKinleys were devout Methodists and founding trustees of the first Methodist Episcopal Church in Niles, and there was a time when the McKinleys hoped that William might join the ministry. But he was more interested in fishing, hunting and engaging in other outdoor activities.

The McKinleys believed strongly in the importance of a good education, and when young William was nine years old, his family moved from Niles to Poland, Ohio, so that the children could enroll in Poland Academy, a local Presbyterian school. While there, William helped found a literary and debate society and particularly enjoyed public speaking. He graduated in 1859 and left home to continue his education at Allegheny College in Meadville, Pennsylvania.

After only a year of college, William became ill and returned home to Ohio. It is unclear exactly what malady he suffered, but by the time William recovered a few months later, his father's business had taken a turn for the worse, and the McKinleys no longer had the resources to finance a college education. Instead, William joined his siblings in the working world. He had a brief stint as a post office clerk and then took a position as a schoolteacher.

CIVIL WAR

William McKinley had not yet completed a year in his new career when the Civil War broke out. Like many young men, the eighteen-year-old answered the call to service. McKinley resigned from his teaching position and enlisted as a private in the Twenty-Third Ohio Volunteer Infantry. He ended up serving under future president and fellow Ohioan Rutherford B. Hayes, who became a friend and mentor.

After training, the Twenty-Third Ohio was sent first to western Virginia and then back toward Washington, where they saw action at the Battle of South Mountain, Maryland. McKinley was assigned to the quartermaster corps and promoted to commissary sergeant with the responsibility of distributing food, clothing and blankets to the troops. On September 17, 1862, he found himself at the Battle of Antietam in Maryland in what would later be known as the bloodiest day of the Civil War. During the battle, McKinley took significant risks to deliver food to troops on the front lines who hadn't eaten all day, providing much-needed sustenance and likely assisting in the Union win. For his bravery, McKinley was promoted to second lieutenant.

In the spring of 1864, the Twenty-Third Ohio was deployed into the Shenandoah Valley, where they participated in the capture of Lexington, Virginia. In July, the two sides met at the Second Battle of Kernstown outside Winchester, Virginia. When it became clear that the Union was not likely to win, McKinley was sent to deliver messages to the front lines to retreat, a risky venture near enemy lines that earned him promotion to captain. He had a horse shot out from under him at the Battle of Berryville in September and saw action at the Battles of Fisher's Hill and Cedar Creek later that fall. By the war's end the following spring, McKinley had been promoted to brevet major for his service in the Shenandoah Valley. He was invited to remain in the professional U.S. Army, but he declined and returned home.

EARLY CAREER

Upon his return to Poland, Ohio, William McKinley decided not to return to his position as a schoolteacher but instead pursue a career in law. He studied under a local attorney and then enrolled in Albany Law School in New York for a year to finish his education. In 1867, he passed the Ohio

William and Ida McKinley, 1894. *Courtesy of the Ohio History Connection (AL00245).*

bar and opened a law office in Canton, about fifty miles southwest of his hometown. As he built his business, McKinley also engaged in civic activities, including leadership roles in the YMCA, local Methodist church and the Republican Party.

At some point, McKinley made the acquaintance of Ida Saxton, eldest daughter of a wealthy Canton businessman and granddaughter of the founder of the local newspaper. Saxton had been educated at private and boarding schools and then took a job as a cashier in her father's bank—something that was still a bit unusual for a wealthy, educated young woman of her time. It was likely at the bank where the two first met. Saxton was initially seeing another young man, but he died suddenly, and after a year-long European tour—which was more common for a young woman of her status—she and McKinley became reacquainted. They were married in January 1871, and her father bought the young couple a house in Canton, where they set about making a home. Their first child, a daughter they named Kate, was born in December of that year. A second daughter, Ida, followed two years later. But shortly thereafter, a series of unfortunate events changed the course of the McKinleys' home life.

Ida Saxton McKinley was by all reports a healthy, confident, smart and hardworking young woman. But just before her second child's birth, Ida's mother, with whom she was very close, died. Then baby Ida was born sickly and died just four months later. Not long after, toddler Kate contracted typhoid fever and died. The shock and grief were too much for Ida to bear, and she apparently suffered a nervous breakdown. Although the details are unclear, Ida was also injured in a fall around the same time that left her bedridden for several months. The cumulative impact of these emotional and physical assaults was such that Ida never fully recovered. For the rest of her life, Ida was plagued with physical and psychological difficulties, including migraine headaches and seizures. William was reportedly a doting husband during this time and, in fact, for the rest of his life. Even as he built himself a political career, he prioritized Ida's needs and organized his schedule to make sure that he was available to her at a moment's notice. Sometimes this involved canceling both social and political activities to help her during the periods when she struggled. The couple never had any additional children.

ROAD TO THE WHITE HOUSE

Despite their traumatic home life, the McKinleys remained focused on William's successful law career and growing political activities. William campaigned for Ohio Republican candidates—including his friend and mentor Rutherford B. Hayes—and successfully represented a group of striking coal miners in a high-profile case, which raised his political standing in both the Republican Party and among voting laborers. In 1876, at the age of thirty-three, McKinley was elected to the U.S. House of Representatives. He initially served with a newly elected President Hayes.

McKinley served in Congress for all but one of the next fourteen years. His most notable accomplishment during this time was shepherding a major tariff bill in his name through Congress: the 1890 McKinley Tariff Bill. It was not universally supported, however, and would eventually cost McKinley his seat in Congress.

Tariffs—taxes placed on the import of foreign-made goods—were the largest source of federal revenue until the ratification of the Sixteenth Amendment in 1913 brought about the widespread implementation of income tax. Debate about which imports should be taxed and at what rate went all the way back to the founding of the United States. Taxes on foreign imports had been as high as 50 percent in the 1820s but settled to around 35 percent for much of the nineteenth century. The McKinley Tariff Bill of 1890—spearheaded by and named after William McKinley—raised the average import tax back up to nearly 50 percent. McKinley's goal was to protect American jobs and manufacturers, although the tariffs also increased the cost of many products used by everyday Americans. Likely as a backlash to the rise in consumer prices, McKinley lost his reelection campaign the year that his eponymous bill became law.

Ousted from the House of Representatives, McKinley returned to Canton and his law practice but quickly took his next step up the political ladder with a run for governor of Ohio in 1891. He won and served two terms. During his time as governor, he focused on trying to mitigate ongoing disagreements between labor and management in Ohio. But he also had his eye on the highest office in the land. With the help of wealthy and politically connected friends, McKinley was nominated as the Republican presidential candidate at the 1896 Republican National Convention on the first ballot. His competition was Democrat William Jennings Bryan.

McKinley's political campaign was a bit of a contradiction. He advocated for the protection of U.S. small businesses and laborers through high foreign

William McKinley during his front porch campaign for U.S. president, 1896. *Courtesy of the Ohio History Connection (AL01079).*

tariffs at the same time that he accepted record political contributions from the very corporations whose unwillingness to negotiate with labor unions was driving down factory wages. The McKinley campaign raised and spent an estimated $3.5 million, exponentially more than any of his predecessors or his competition. This money was spent largely on printing and mailings. Very little was spent on travel because, like several of his predecessors, McKinley spent most of his campaign at home. While Bryan traveled across the country, sometimes delivering multiple speeches a day, McKinley conducted a carefully scripted "front porch" campaign. Selected groups of supporters were invited to visit his Canton home for supportive speeches and rallies. And like other Ohioans before him, McKinley's approach was successful. In the November 1896 presidential election, McKinley won both the popular and electoral votes. He and Ida packed up and relocated to Washington the following spring.

PRESIDENCY

William McKinley's presidential campaign had largely focused on internal concerns—specifically the economy and tariffs. However, circumstances were such that international affairs consumed most of McKinley's attention during his time in the White House. By the end of his presidency, the United States had expanded its territorial power into the Caribbean, Pacific Ocean and east Asia and, for better or worse, had become a leader on the world stage. McKinley did not set out for this to happen; many of the issues that came to a head during his presidency had been brewing for many years.

First up was a crisis in Cuba, a longtime Spanish colony. Cubans had been agitating for independence for many years. The conflict reached a crisis in 1895 with the Cuban War of Independence. This war threatened U.S. business interests in Cuba, and the political instability felt particularly close to the southern U.S. border. McKinley sympathized with the Cuban rebels—as did most Americans—but he didn't really want the United States to go to war with Spain. Instead, he attempted to negotiate with Spain for Cuba's freedom, which was largely unsuccessful. Meanwhile, American businesses interests agitated for U.S. involvement to protect their investments in Cuba. In January 1898, McKinley sent the battleship USS *Maine* to Havana Harbor, largely in hopes that an American presence would calm down the conflict. A month later, the USS *Maine* exploded, and 266 people were killed. An investigation by the U.S. Navy determined that the ship was sunk by an underwater mine, although subsequent investigations cast doubt on that determination. Even though there was no clear proof of who set the mine, many in the United States agitated for retaliation. In April, with McKinley's support, Congress declared war on Spain.

The Spanish-American War lasted just four months but resulted in Spain losing the last of its colonies to the United States. The United States sent both naval and ground forces into Cuba and Puerto Rico, also a Spanish colony, to force out the Spanish military. The U.S. Navy also attacked the Spanish presence in the Philippines, where a group of Filipino nationalists had been fighting against Spanish occupation for years. Although initially allied, the Filipino nationalists were no happier with the presence of the U.S. military than they were with the Spanish, and the United States ended up fighting against the same population that they claimed to be liberating.

In the end, Spain was defeated and for $20 million turned over to the United States possession of Guam, Puerto Rico and the Philippines and temporary ownership of Cuba. The United States set up military governments in both Cuba and the Philippines with the goal of eventually transitioning the nations to self-government, while also solidifying the United States' political and economic influence in the Caribbean and Asia. Cuba would eventually gain its independence in 1902; the Philippines wouldn't gain full independence until the end of World War II.

Amid the conflicts, Congress approved the annexation of another strategic island nation: Hawaii. The native Queen Lili'uokalani had been overthrown in 1893 by a group of insurgents backed by U.S. businessmen. They wanted the island nation to become part of the United States to provide better access to trade in Asia, but Congress initially objected to the illegal coup d'état and refused to approve the annexation. Pressure mounted during McKinley's presidency, and Hawaii was finally annexed in July 1898.

Until the late nineteenth century, China was still largely closed to foreign trade, much to the chagrin of businessmen from around the world who saw a giant untapped market for factory-produced goods. Beginning in the 1890s, Japan, Russia and European nations began slowly establishing trade relations with China. U.S. businessmen wanted to get in on the action and pressured the McKinley administration to make sure the United States wasn't left out of any trade agreements. McKinley authorized his secretary of state to release a statement that the United States believed that all countries should have unrestricted access, or an "open door," to trade with China. This did not go over well with a group of Chinese nationalists, known as the Boxers, who wanted to keep foreign influence out of China. In June 1900, the Boxers attacked a group of foreign missionaries in an attempt to force them to leave and discourage future foreign activity. In response, McKinley sent U.S. troops to help put down what came to be known as the Boxer Rebellion. By the end of the summer, the Boxers had been subdued, and China was effectively forced open to foreign trade.

By the time of McKinley's reelection campaign in late 1900, big changes were happening on the homefront. Immigration, urbanization and industrialization of the United States continued at a rapid pace while big business continued to have more and more power over political, social and economic life. The spread of slums, rampant child labor and the use of violence against labor strikers was so widespread that it could no longer be ignored. Writers and photographers such as Ida Tarbell, Upton Sinclair, Jacob Riis and Lewis Hine exposed the corruption in politics, lack of regulation in big business and the plight of the poor in newspapers and magazines that reached more people than ever before. Middle-class

William McKinley at his desk, 1897. *Photograph by Frances Benjamin Johnston. Library of Congress, Prints and Photographs Division.*

Americans began demanding change and organizing social and political reform efforts ranging from prohibition to food regulation to settlement houses to election reform.

The man McKinley selected for his second-term running mate would later become known for embracing the Progressive Era reforms that were bubbling up in American culture: Spanish-American War hero and New York governor Theodore Roosevelt. The Republican Party again spent millions of dollars on the McKinley-Roosevelt campaign, and the Republicans defeated Democrat William Jennings Bryan for a second time.

ASSASSINATION

Throughout William McKinley's political career, he juggled his official obligations with caretaking of Ida, whose symptoms ebbed and flowed over the years. When he was home, William arranged his schedule so that he could check in with her throughout the day. When he traveled, he made sure that she was cared for by family or friends and wrote to her every day. Ida was given a variety of medications to try to manage her seizures and melancholy, but they sometimes made her behavior erratic or even violent. When protocol required the first lady's presence, but staff were unsure if she could manage, Ida was sometimes sedated and propped in a chair with a bouquet of flowers in her hands and then whisked off as soon as possible. During formal dinners, William would arrange to have Ida seated next to him so that if she had a seizure, he could place a napkin over her head to grant privacy until it was over. Without modern medical treatment or, in fact, much understanding of her challenges, Ida was largely left to cope as best as possible.

In 1900, Ida entered a period when she particularly struggled with her mental and physical health. Despite their concerns, the McKinleys embarked on a cross-country train trip shortly after his March 1901 inauguration. The trip was supposed to end in June with a visit to the Pan-American Exposition in Buffalo, New York. However, Ida fell ill while they were in California, and they were unable to continue. They cut short the rest of their trip and returned to Washington.

By September, Ida was feeling better, and the McKinleys finally made their way to Buffalo. They did not know that there was another attendee at the Pan-American Exposition who came with ulterior motives. Leon Czolgosz was a twenty-eight-year-old from Detroit, Michigan, the son of Polish immigrants and a factory worker who struggled to find steady work after the economic crash of 1893. Czolgosz became increasingly disillusioned with the American political system and enamored with anarchist ideas. He bought a .32-caliber revolver and made his way to Buffalo with the intent to kill the president.

On September 6, McKinley was greeting visitors in a receiving line at the exposition. Czolgosz made his way through the receiving line, and when he reached McKinley, he shot the president twice in the abdomen. While McKinley collapsed, the Secret Service immediately captured and arrested Czolgosz.

McKinley did not die immediately from his wounds. He was taken to a hospital on the grounds of the exposition where doctors discovered that the first shot had not done any damage, but the second had gone through his stomach and was believed to be lodged somewhere behind his pancreas. The doctors knew that poking around in his abdomen would likely cause more damage—it had resulted in the untimely death of President James A. Garfield twenty years before—so they sewed McKinley up and sent him off to rest and recuperate.

For the first few days, it looked like McKinley would recover. He was able to speak and eat broth by the fourth day. But on the sixth day, he took a turn for the worse. Doctors didn't yet know, but the bullet had punctured his pancreas. McKinley died on September 14, 1901.

Czolgosz was tried and convicted of first-degree murder in Buffalo. He was executed in October 1901.

WILLIAM MCKINLEY HISTORIC SITES IN OHIO

McKinley Birthplace Home
40 South Main Street, Niles, OH
330-652-1704
mcklib.org/BirthplaceHome

William McKinley was born in a small eight-room house in Niles, Ohio, on January 29, 1843. When William was nine years old, the family moved, and the house passed through several owners. In 1890, the land on which the house was situated was needed for the construction of a bank. A person whose name is lost to time financed cutting the McKinley house in half, and the portion in which the future president had been born was moved to Riverside Park, a local amusement park, where it served as an early museum attraction. When the amusement park went out of business, the house was rented out to tenants. In 1909, a local resident purchased the house, reunited it with its other half and moved both onto her property, where she operated a private museum. Eventually, the building fell into disrepair and was torn or burned down in the 1930s.

In 1994, the bank that occupied the home's original location donated the land to the City of Niles. The city tore down the bank building and, in 2002, began construction of a replica of the original house where McKinley was born. The replica house, dedicated the following year, also contains a library of McKinley-related material.

The McKinley Birthplace Home is currently operated by the McKinley Memorial Library and is open seasonally. Admission is free.

National McKinley Birthplace Memorial Museum
40 North Main Street, Niles, OH
330-652-4273
mckinleybirthplacemuseum.org

The National McKinley Birthplace Memorial Museum is located just down the street from the McKinley Birthplace Home and adjacent to the public library that bears McKinley's name. The site was selected and developed by a childhood friend of McKinley's on the site of the one-room schoolhouse that the future president attended as a child. The Beaux Arts–style marble building was designed by the architectural firm of McKim, Mead and White, best known for having designed New York's Penn Station and the Boston Public Library. The museum was dedicated in 1917 by President William Taft.

National McKinley Birthplace Memorial Museum in Niles, Ohio. *Author's collection.*

The first floor of the museum is an open hall designed for public events and features changing exhibits. The second floor holds exhibits about McKinley's life and presidency and has both campaign memorabilia and family items, including a piano, rocking chair and desk. Featured throughout the museum and the outside memorial are fifty-two bronze busts of businessmen, politicians and industrialists who contributed either to McKinley's political work or to fundraising for the museum.

The National McKinley Birthplace Memorial Museum is open Tuesday through Friday. Admission is free.

McKinley Presidential Library and Museum
800 McKinley Monument Drive NW, Canton, OH
330-455-7043
mckinleymuseum.org

The McKinley Presidential Library and Museum is a combination history and science museum and holds the largest collection of McKinley artifacts that are available to the public. It is an innovative and family-friendly approach to a presidential museum.

Upon entrance to the museum, a small exhibit tells the story of McKinley's life. Visitors can also view a video about the construction of the nearby McKinley National Memorial. Following is a gallery about the two-hundred-year history of Stark County, with a particular focus on inventions and industrial innovations that took place in Canton and surrounding areas.

The McKinley Gallery is the exhibit room where the presidential collection is on display. Animatronic figures of Ida and William McKinley welcome visitors and tell brief stories about their lives. The collection includes several pieces of furniture that belonged to the McKinleys, as well as personal items such as Ida's crochet bag and one of the many pairs of slippers that she crocheted for friends, supporters and to auction off as fundraisers. The exhibit also tells the stories of how a few of the recent pieces were acquired, which provides a bit of a behind-the-scenes peek at museum operations.

The remainder of the main floor of the museum is composed of a "Street of Shops"—a recreation of a nineteenth-century main street, including a general store, saloon, toy store, print shop, doctor's office and blacksmith shop. Visitors can enter several of the re-created spaces and hear recorded stories about life at that time. There is also a large model railroad depicting historic sites in Stark County.

Animatronic Ida and William McKinley at the McKinley Presidential Library and Museum. *Courtesy of the McKinley Presidential Library and Museum.*

The lower level of the museum is composed of a science center. Exhibits include dinosaurs and archaeological artifacts, natural history displays and a technology area with hands-on activities. There is also a planetarium that offers daily astronomy programs.

The library portion of the facility is the Ramsayer Research Center, which contains books, periodicals and archival material related to the McKinleys and the history of Stark County. It is open by appointment.

The McKinley Presidential Library and Museum is owned and operated by the Stark County Historical Society. The museum is open Tuesday through Saturday, and an admission is charged.

McKinley "Campaign" House
723 North Market Street, Canton, OH

The house where William McKinley launched his "front porch" campaign for president is no longer standing. The Stark County District Library is now at that address, and a historical marker identifies the site.

Saxton-McKinley House
First Ladies National Historic Site
205 Market Avenue South, Canton, OH
330-452-0876
nps.gov/fila

Ida Saxton, future wife of William McKinley, was born in Canton, Ohio. She and her two siblings were raised in an 1841 Victorian home that was originally owned by their grandfather. Ida's sister remained in the home and raised her own children there. After the loss of their infant daughter, Ida and William McKinley moved into the Canton home with Ida's sister and her family. They resided on the third floor, where William also had his law office.

The Saxton-McKinley House remained in the Saxton family until 1919. Over the years, the building was converted to apartments, a restaurant, a barbershop and even a brothel. In 1998, the Saxton-McKinley House became the home of the National First Ladies Library, and the house was restored and reconstructed to represent its Victorian-era roots. It is now part of the First Ladies National Historic Site and is operated by the National Park Service. Guided tours take visitors through a reconstructed parlor, dining room and library, and exhibits in other rooms tell the story of McKinley's presidential campaign. There are a few objects in the house that belonged to the McKinleys, including a piano, a music box, some jewelry and a gown.

Also part of the First Ladies National Historic Site is an Education Center with changing exhibits on the first ladies. A vintage theater also shows videos about the first ladies.

The First Ladies National Historic Site is open Tuesday through Saturday (hours vary in the winter), with guided tours of the Saxton-McKinley House offered three times per day. The Education Center is free; a fee is charged for tours of the house.

McKinley National Memorial
800 McKinley Monument Drive NW, Canton, OH
330-455-7043

After his death, William McKinley's remains were placed in a temporary vault while funds were raised for the creation of a permanent memorial. The McKinley National Monument Association set a goal to raise $600,000 for the memorial. Children donated their pennies, and banks and postal carriers

McKinley National Memorial in Canton, Ohio. *Courtesy of the McKinley Presidential Library and Museum.*

across the country were authorized to collect donations. Construction of the monument began in 1905 on land purchased from West Lawn Cemetery. Supplies and workers from around the country were brought in to construct the brick and marble structure, and it was dedicated in September 1907.

The memorial is composed of a large dome that sits at the center of a cross and overlooking what is intended to represent a sword. Originally, the sword included a water feature, but it was removed in the 1950s. In front of the memorial is a large bronze sculpture of McKinley as he appeared while giving his last speech, shortly before he was shot. The McKinleys and their two daughters are interred within.

The McKinley National Memorial is owned and operated by the Stark County Historical Society. The monument is open daily from April to November and is free.

WILLIAM HOWARD TAFT

Our Twenty-Seventh President

FAST FACTS ABOUT WILLIAM HOWARD TAFT

- Twenty-seventh president of the United States
- Born on September 15, 1857; died on March 8, 1930
- Served one term: 1909–13
- Married Helen Herron (1861–1943) in 1886
- Children: Robert Alphonso (1889–1953), Helen Herron (1891–1987) and Charles Phelps (1897–1983)
- First president to own a car
- Only person to serve as both president and chief justice
- Prior careers: lawyer, judge, governor of the Philippines, secretary of war
- Subsequent careers: professor, U.S. Supreme Court justice

ALL ABOUT WILLIAM HOWARD TAFT

William Howard Taft never really wanted to be president. His dream was to be a Supreme Court justice, but family pressure detoured him away from law and into the world of politics. After positions in state and federal courts, as governor of the Philippines and as secretary of war, Taft was elected vice

Right: William H. Taft, circa 1908. *Library of Congress, Prints and Photographs Division.*

Opposite: William H. Taft (*seated center*) and classmates at the Woodward High School, circa 1878–74. *Library of Congress, Prints and Photographs Division.*

president under Theodore Roosevelt in 1904. Roosevelt groomed Taft to take his place in the White House and then turned against him when Taft failed to carry out Roosevelt's reform efforts, forcing Taft out of office after just one term. Finally, at the age of sixty-three, Taft received his longed-for appointment, making him the only person to serve as both U.S. president and chief justice of the U.S. Supreme Court.

EARLY LIFE

William Howard Taft was born on September 15, 1857, in Cincinnati, Ohio. His father, Alphonso Taft, was originally from Vermont and moved to Ohio as a young man to pursue a career as an attorney. Alphonso married a fellow Vermonter who bore him five children—only two who survived infancy—and then died of tuberculosis. Alphonso went back to New England to find a stepmother for his two young sons and returned to Cincinnati with Louise

Torrey. Louise was born in Boston and graduated from Mount Holyoke Female Seminary. She worked as a schoolteacher before marrying, and the advancement of education remained important throughout her life. There was an almost twenty-year age difference between the couple, but the two were apparently devoted to their blended family.

The first child of Louise and Alphonso Taft did not survive infanthood, but their second was a healthy and hearty baby boy whom they named William Howard and called Willie. They then had two additional boys, followed by a girl—bringing the total number of Taft children to five boys and one girl. They lived with Alphonso's parents in a large house on a hilltop in a well-to-do neighborhood overlooking the city of Cincinnati.

Alphonso was a successful attorney, then judge and eventually served as President Ulysses S. Grant's secretary of war and as a minister to Austria-Hungary and Russia. The family was among the most prominent in Cincinnati, and they had several staff working for them at the house, often young immigrants for whom domestic work was a step up from the factory work available along the city waterfront. The family were originally New England Baptists but converted to the Unitarian Universalist Church when Willie was a child. Both Alphonso and Louise were believers in the importance of education and civil engagement. They raised money for the construction of the first reform school in Cincinnati, built to keep wayward youngsters out of the local jail and give them a second chance.

The Tafts were also fierce abolitionists and supported freedom of religion. In 1872, when Willie was a teenager and perhaps just old enough to pay attention to his father's politics, Alphonso dissented against a judicial ruling that would have forced the reading of the Bible in public, arguing instead in support of religious freedom in public schools.

Willie was a chunky child; his friends called him "Big Lub." But he loved baseball, boxing and horseback riding. He was also a good student and attended the local high school, graduating as salutatorian in 1874. Like his father, Willie went on to study at Yale College, where he was a hardworking student and wresting champion. He graduated second in his class in 1878 and then enrolled at Cincinnati Law School, where he graduated two years later.

EARLY CAREER

In 1880, William Howard Taft passed the Ohio bar and went to work as a prosecuting attorney for Hamilton County. He took on extra work as election supervisor for the state and collector of internal revenue for the City of Cincinnati. Within a few years, he was running his own law firm.

Shortly thereafter, William began dating the daughter of another local attorney—Helen "Nellie" Herron. Nellie had grown up in a large, prominent and politically connected family in Cincinnati. She was educated in private schools and at Miami University in Ohio. Balking against the social expectations of upper-class women of her time, Nellie had initially hoped to have a career rather than marriage. She worked in her father's law office, taught French classes and yearned to leave Ohio. She also started a literary society in Cincinnati, and it was there that she got to know William. He proposed several times before she eventually accepted.

The couple married on June 19, 1886, and settled in Cincinnati. They moved into a house in a wealthy Cincinnati neighborhood that was gifted to them by Nellie's family and eventually had three children.

Nellie was ambitious and, in a period when there were few career options for women, directed her energies toward pushing William to build his career. She had visited the White House as a child and dreamed of returning as a first lady. It was she who encouraged William to build on his family and business connections to pursue higher-level positions and enter the world of politics.

At his heart, William loved the law and rose quickly through the ranks. He served as judge in Cincinnati Superior Court and then spent two years in Washington, D.C., as U.S. solicitor general, arguing cases on behalf of the federal government in front of the U.S. Supreme Court. In 1892, President Benjamin Harrison appointed him judge in the Sixth U.S. Court of Appeals, hearing cases from a four-state region. William also taught law classes at his alma mater and hoped that his next move might be a permanent one to Washington with an appointment to the U.S. Supreme Court. Nellie, too, enjoyed life in Washington and worked to build connections that might help her family remain there.

By 1900, Taft had come to the attention of President William McKinley, but the job McKinley offered was not the one that Taft wanted. Under McKinley, the United States had won the Spanish-American War and found itself with several new island nations to manage. McKinley asked Taft to head a commission that would determine what to do with the newly acquired Philippine Islands. Taft was not keen to move into politics or live abroad, but McKinley urged that it would be a good career move and put Taft in line for the next open seat on the U.S. Supreme Court. With that promise and Nellie's encouragement, he accepted the position.

The United States had won the Philippine Islands from Spain, but there was an active group of local nationalists who fought occupation by any colonial power. As the U.S. military fought to put down the rebellion, Taft was given the task of creating a civilian government and developing a plan for transforming the Philippines into a U.S.-friendly self-governed nation. His time in the Philippines was largely successful: he stabilized the

William H. Taft and his family on their front porch, circa 1909. *Library of Congress, Prints and Photographs Division.*

economy, built schools and hospitals and drafted a national constitution modeled after the U.S. Constitution. He also negotiated the purchase of land from the Roman Catholic Church and redistributed it to poor Filipinos, earning him the respect of local residents.

While they were abroad, President McKinley was assassinated and his vice president, Theodore Roosevelt, stepped into the presidency. Twice Roosevelt offered Taft a seat on the U.S. Supreme Court, but both times Taft declined. He felt he still had work to do in the Philippines, and Nellie loved their life abroad. They lived on a large estate with a thirty-five-room palace, hosted lavish events and traveled throughout Asia.

In 1903, Roosevelt made Taft another job offer, this time as secretary of war—a position once held by Taft's father. Taft agreed, in large part because as head of the War Department he would be able to continue engagement with the islands. The Tafts packed their bags in December and headed back to Washington.

ROAD TO THE WHITE HOUSE

Back in Washington, William Howard Taft quickly became Theodore Roosevelt's invaluable right-hand man and protege. In addition to Taft running the War Department and serving as a cabinet advisor, Roosevelt set him on several handpicked projects that would give Taft additional experience and attention both at home and abroad.

In 1904, Roosevelt put Taft in charge of plans to build what would become the Panama Canal. Business and political interests in the United States wanted to find a way to cut down the time and expense of shipping to the West Coast by constructing a canal over the Isthmus of Panama to link the Atlantic and Pacific Oceans. It was the largest engineering project undertaken by the United States until that time and required understanding both the logistics of canal building and transportation as well as navigating the complicated politics of Central America. Taft also had to figure out how to keep the canal laborers working, as yellow fever and malaria sickened thousands, threatening the completion of the project. At a particularly pivotal moment, Taft recruited Dr. William C. Gorgas, an expert in battling tropical disease, who implemented new sanitation programs and drained standing water that bred the mosquitos that transmitted the diseases, allowing the project to continue. This would later serve as a model for future public health and sanitation efforts.

When fighting broke out in Cuba in 1906 after a disputed election, Roosevelt sent Taft there to calm the conflict and serve as provisional governor. Cuba had been acquired by the United States after the Spanish-American War, but the United States had fairly quickly given the nation its independence. Part of the treaty agreement, however, gave the United States power to step in and run the country on a temporary basis if there were ever threats to the nation's stability. Taft remained in Cuba for less than a month, at which time he passed the governorship to another American diplomat. New elections were held, and after a new Cuban president took office in 1909, U.S. troops withdrew.

This political cartoon, which appeared in *Puck* on March 4, 1908, shows President Theodore Roosevelt as the real force behind the presidential candidacy of William H. Taft. Basketball had been developed just sixteen years earlier. *Cartoonist Frank Nankivell. Library of Congress, Prints and Photographs Division.*

Roosevelt also sent Taft on diplomatic trips to the Philippines and Japan. On several occasions, William took Nellie and one or two of his children with him, and the cost of the trips drew the criticism of Congress and the newspapers. Taft avoided controversy by asking his wealthy brother Charlie to help fund his travel, removing the expenses from the federal coffers.

Meanwhile, things were changing on the homefront. Roosevelt was a dynamic, engaging and immensely popular president who spent his time in office bringing about the Progressive Era reforms that his predecessors had struggled to enact for several decades. At a time when the media was bringing more attention than ever to the plights of the poor and disadvantaged, Roosevelt believed in using the power of the federal government to improve everyday life. He fought back against big corporations that had unfair labor practices, pushed for laws that provided consumer protections on food and drugs, intervened in labor disputes and advocated for the preservation of natural resources.

Roosevelt had stepped into the presidency after William McKinley's assassination in 1901. When he was elected three years later, Roosevelt pledged not to run for another term, a promise he lived to regret. As the 1908 election season rolled around, however, Roosevelt decided the next best thing to a third term in office would be to select and groom his successor. And the man he selected was Taft.

Taft was lukewarm, at best, about the prospect of leading the nation. Nellie, on the other hand, saw the possibility of her childhood dream finally coming true. The rest of Taft's extended family was also thrilled about the prospect. Taft reluctantly let them, and Roosevelt, persuade him to run for president—something he, too, would live to regret.

With Roosevelt's support, Taft was nominated on the first ballot at the Republican National Convention in June 1908. James Sherman, a senator from New York, was selected as his running mate. His rival was Democrat William Jennings Bryan, running for the presidency for the third time.

Taft did not enjoy public speaking but resigned from his position as secretary of war and took to the road. His campaign promises were largely to carry on Roosevelt's reform efforts: ending monopolies in business and industry, regulating the railroads and conserving natural resources. With the support of Roosevelt and both the conservative and progressive branches of the Republican Party, Taft easily won the presidential election.

William H. Taft talking on the telephone as he receives news of his nomination as the 1908 Republican presidential candidate. *Photograph by Harris & Ewing. Library of Congress, Prints and Photographs Division.*

PRESIDENT

William Howard Taft took office as president in March 1909, and quickly it became clear that he was not interested in following blindly in his predecessor's footsteps. Where Theodore Roosevelt was outgoing and outspoken and pushed the boundaries of his role as president, Taft was more moderate and focused on making the federal government work more efficiently and effectively. While Roosevelt would later criticize Taft for not being progressive enough, he did carry out several important reforms.

During his time in office, Taft restructured the State Department, organizing it into geographic departments, and instituted reforms in the U.S. Post Office that made it self-supporting for the first time. Taft also strengthened the regulation of railroads and forced the breakup of several trusts, allowing smaller businesses greater access to the free market. Also during Taft's presidency, the United States added ten national parks and the states of New Mexico and Arizona.

As with previous U.S. presidents, foreign tariffs played a large role in Taft's presidency. For decades, the Republican Party had generally advocated for high tariffs to protect U.S. manufacturers. By Taft's presidency, however, this had begun to change. As mass-produced consumer products became more available, Americans balked at the high prices that came with foreign imports. Taft had promised during his campaign to reform tariffs, but he signed a bill—the 1909 Payne-Aldrich Tariff bill—that made only slight modifications. Taft also found himself on the wrong side of public opinion when he objected to instituting federal income tax, something that would be ratified in 1913 as the Sixteenth Amendment to the U.S. Constitution.

On the foreign affairs arena, Taft focused his policy on what he called "dollar diplomacy": using U.S. political and military power to promote U.S. business interests internationally. His administration was particularly focused on keeping European economic and political influence out of South and Central America, something that was largely unsuccessful.

During their first year in the White House, Nellie suffered a stroke that left her incapacitated for several months. Their daughter, Helen, took a year off from college and came to Washington to serve as White House hostess. Nellie recovered, however, in time to celebrate their silver wedding anniversary at the White House. She also arranged that a gift of more than three thousand cherry trees from the mayor of Tokyo, Japan, be planted around the Tidal Basin near the Jefferson Memorial, where they remain today.

Roosevelt, who had spent most of Taft's first year in office out of the country, returned in 1910 and was not happy with the situation in Washington. He thought that Taft had allowed the more conservative branch of the Republican Party to gain power and was not pushing for the reforms that Roosevelt had begun. He also accused Taft of thwarting Roosevelt's conservation policies when Taft fired the head of the U.S. Forest Service, a friend of Roosevelt's. By the end of the year, Roosevelt had begun speaking out publicly against his successor.

When the 1912 election season rolled around, Roosevelt had changed his mind and challenged Taft for the Republican Party nomination. Heading into the Republican National Convention, it looked like Roosevelt might be nominated, but the conservative Republicans supported Taft instead. When Roosevelt lost the Republication nomination, he created the Progressive Party to run against both Taft and the Democratic candidate, Woodrow Wilson. Taft had neither the political support nor the finances to actively campaign for a second term, and the Republican vote was divided between

"IS THAT THE BEST CARE YOU COULD TAKE OF MY CAT?"

This political cartoon, which appeared in *Puck* on March 27, 1912, is titled "Is that the best care you could take of my cat?" and depicts Teddy Roosevelt looking horrified at how William H. Taft has taken care of his cat, labeled "my policies," during his absence. *Library of Congress, Prints and Photographs Division.*

Roosevelt and Taft. Wilson easily won the election, and Taft came in third with just eight electoral votes.

POST-PRESIDENCY LIFE

It was with some relief that William Howard Taft packed his bags to leave the White House in the spring of 1913. Rather than returning to Ohio, however, the Tafts moved to Connecticut, where William took a job teaching at Yale University Law School. During Woodrow Wilson's presidency, Taft served as president of the American Bar Association and wrote for both legal and popular publications.

In 1921, at long last, Taft received the appointment to the position that he had yearned for since the beginning of his career. President Warren G. Harding appointed him as chief justice of the U.S. Supreme Court,

William H. Taft as chief justice of the U.S. Supreme Court, circa 1921–30. *Photograph by Harris & Ewing. Library of Congress, Prints and Photographs Division.*

making him the only person to serve as head of two branches of the federal government. During his time as chief justice, Taft worked to modernize the U.S. Supreme Court by advocating for reform that allowed the court to decide which cases to hear. His decisions on cases tended toward conservativism and limiting the power of government, although he also ruled in favor of laws that prohibited child labor and set a minimum wage for women. In 1929, Taft persuaded Congress to fund the building of a separate U.S. Supreme Court building, which was completed after his death.

Taft's health declined in the last few years of his life. He resigned from the U.S. Supreme Court in February 1930 due to illness. He died from complications of heart disease on March 8 at the age of seventy-two. He was buried in Arlington National Cemetery.

WILLIAM HOWARD TAFT HISTORIC SITES IN OHIO

William Howard Taft National Historic Site

2038 Auburn Avenue, Cincinnati, OH
513-684-3263
nps.gov/wiho

The house where William Howard Taft grew up was purchased by his father, Alphonso, in Mount Auburn, which was then a well-to-do Cincinnati suburb. Alphonso expanded the Greek Revival house to accommodate his growing family, including six children and a set of grandparents. The house was originally built in the 1840s and sat on almost two acres of hilltop land overlooking the Ohio River.

William lived in the house until he left for college in 1874. The family rented the house out while Alphonso served in Washington and then relocated to California. The Taft family eventually sold the house in 1899, and it passed through several owners and was converted into apartments. In the 1950s, the William Howard Taft Memorial Association, led by William's son, purchased the house back to save it from demolition. In 1969, the house became part of the National Park Service, which operates it today. A comprehensive restoration of the house was completed in the 1980s.

The site is composed of a welcome center and the Taft family house. The house is open by guided tour, which takes visitors through several rooms on the first floor that have been restored to appear as they did in the 1860s.

A museum exhibit inside the William Howard Taft National Historic Site. *Author's collection.*

Some rooms contain items that belonged to the Tafts; the remainder are period pieces. Rooms on the second floor of the house contain exhibits about Taft's life and career.

The William Howard Taft National Historic Site is open daily. Admission is free.

WILLIAM HOWARD TAFT HISTORIC SITES OUTSIDE OF OHIO

Arlington National Cemetery
Arlington, VA
877-907-8585
arlingtoncemetery.mil

William Howard Taft was the first president to be buried in Arlington National Cemetery. Nellie selected the site where her husband was to be buried in what was then an undeveloped section of the cemetery. His headstone was designed by American sculptor James Earle Fraser, who also designed the National Archives and U.S. Supreme Court buildings in Washington, D.C.

WARREN G. HARDING

OUR TWENTY-NINTH PRESIDENT

FAST FACTS ABOUT WARREN G. HARDING

- Twenty-ninth president of the United States
- Born on November 2, 1865; died on August 2, 1923
- Served from 1921–23
- Married Florence Mabel Kling (1860–1924) in 1891
- Stepson: Marshall Eugene DeWolfe (1880–1915)
- First president to have a radio in the White House
- Prior careers: teacher, newspaper publisher, politician
- His was the first U.S. presidential election that allowed women to vote

ALL ABOUT WARREN G. HARDING

Warren G. Harding came to the U.S. presidency from a different career path than his peers: he was a newspaperman before becoming a politician. As a result, he had a particularly good understanding of the media in an age when it was becoming more influential than ever before. He used this to his advantage in his presidential campaign and had a more open relationship with reporters during his presidency than any of his predecessors. His

Warren G. Harding, circa 1920. *Library of Congress, Prints and Photographs Division.*

connections also likely kept unfavorable reports about Harding out of the press until after his death. Like two of his fellow Ohio presidents, Harding's time in the White House was cut short before its completion. He died of a heart attack not quite two and a half years into his term, bringing to an end the run of Buckeye presidents.

EARLY YEARS

Warren Gamaliel Harding was born on November 2, 1865, in what is now Blooming Grove, Ohio, the first child of George Tryon Harding and Phoebe Dickerson Harding. The couple had married just before George enlisted in the Union army to fight in the Civil War. George was discharged with typhoid fever in late 1864 and returned to Blooming Grove to teach school. The couple had eight children, six of whom survived to adulthood. When Warren was a toddler, his parents began studying homeopathic medicine, and eventually, his father became a country doctor and his mother a midwife.

Warren was raised in a home that valued education and the arts. His mother taught him to read before he entered school, and his father, who had played the fife and drums in the Union army, instilled in him a love of music. When Warren was young, the Hardings moved to the small village of Caledonia, Ohio. There, he attended a one-room schoolhouse, played the horn in a local band and had a typical rural childhood with his younger siblings. At some point, his father came to be part owner of a local newspaper—apparently as payment for a debt—and Warren worked there part time for a year or two to earn pocket money. It was a small job but launched Warren's lifelong love of the newspaper business.

In 1879, Warren enrolled in Ohio Central College in Iberia, Ohio. He particularly enjoyed his English classes and became founding editor of the student newspaper. He graduated three years later. While he was at college, his family moved to the county seat of Marion, Ohio, and upon graduation, Warren joined them.

THE NEWSPAPER BUSINESS

Seventeen-year-old Warren G. Harding had no clear career plans upon graduation from college. He tried teaching school, briefly studied law, started a band and sold insurance—none of which captured the young man's passions. This all changed in 1884 when one of the three local newspapers, the *Marion Star*, came up for auction. Harding raised $300 with two friends and purchased the failing newspaper, appointing himself both editor and publisher. One of the first big stories that Harding covered for the newspaper was the June 1884 Republican National Convention in Chicago. This would have been an exciting event for a young reporter and gave Harding his first taste for the world of politics. Soon after, Harding bought out his partners and became sole owner and publisher of the *Marion Star*. He continued in this role until shortly before his death.

After some initial hiccups, the *Marion Star* took off. By 1890, it was the only daily newspaper in Marion and played an important role in both reporting the local news and advocating for improvement of the growing town. The newspaper's editorial page called for the electrification of the city, encouraged the building of a local theater or opera house and urged

Warren G. Harding setting type at the *Marion Star*, the newspaper he owned, 1920. *Courtesy of the Ohio History Connection (P146_B20_P8_02_B33).*

the municipal government to pave streets. Harding's editorials also often criticized a local real estate speculator and banker named Amos H. Kling—the wealthiest man in town and father of the woman who would later become Harding's wife.

Florence Mabel Kling was born in August 1860 in Marion, Ohio. She was the eldest child and apparently inherited the strong will that made her father, Amos Kling, so successful in business. Florence was a talented musician and studied piano at the Cincinnati Conservatory of Music for two years. On holidays back home, however, she often clashed with her father. At age nineteen, Florence eloped and moved to Columbus, Ohio, where she gave birth to a son. By the time the boy was two years old, his father had abandoned the small family. Left destitute and with no support, Florence and her son moved back to Marion. Amos refused to take in his daughter and grandson, so she lived with a friend and taught piano lessons to help pay the bills. After some time, Amos offered to take in his grandson and raise him as his own child; Florence agreed. The mother and son remained in touch but were not close.

It was while giving piano lessons to his sister that Florence met Warren. They began dating in 1886 and were engaged in 1890. Despite their estrangement, Amos Kling was livid at the prospect of his daughter marrying a lowly newspaperman and did everything he could to prevent the union. Kling made public threats against Harding, bought up Harding's father's debts in an attempt to bankrupt him and started rumors that Harding's ancestors were Black—a deep insult for people of Harding's race and status at the time. The young couple was not dissuaded, however, and married on July 8, 1891. They had no children together.

The couple were reportedly a case of opposites attracting. Florence was organized and demanding, Warren more laidback. His nickname for her was "The Boss"; hers for him was "Sonny." Troubled by chronic health problems, Warren would regularly take respite at a sanitarium in Michigan to recuperate from stress and what is now believed to be a long-standing and undiagnosed heart condition. During one such visit in 1894, the business manager of the *Marion Star* quit, and Florence stepped in to take charge. She quickly became indispensable to the running of the newspaper. Although she never held an official title, Florence took on the tasks of wrangling the crew of young newsboys, managing the circulation department and keeping the newspaper's books. She is also credited with hiring the first female reporter in Ohio. Ever on the lookout for possible opportunities, Florence was also the one who encouraged her husband to enter the world of politics.

ROAD TO THE WHITE HOUSE

The Hardings were supporters of the Republican Party, and Warren campaigned for fellow Ohioan William McKinley in his 1896 presidential campaign. In 1899, Harding made his own run for political office and was elected to the Ohio State Senate. He was reelected two years later and then elected lieutenant governor of Ohio the following year. Harding took a hiatus in 1905 to care for Florence, who was very ill from a genetic kidney defect, but resumed his political career upon her recovery.

In 1910, Harding lost a run for governor of Ohio but remained a player in Republican politics. Two years later, President William H. Taft asked Harding to speak in his support at the 1912 Republican National Convention, where Taft was facing a challenge by former president Theodore Roosevelt. Taft won the nomination; Roosevelt launched his own political party, and both lost to Democrat Woodrow Wilson later that fall.

The following year, Florence encouraged Warren to run for the U.S. Senate. Thanks to the Seventeenth Amendment, U.S. senators were newly selected by election rather than legislative appointment. Harding won, becoming the first senator in Ohio elected by direct election, and the couple relocated to Washington, D.C. Harding's congressional career was uneventful, and he missed several key votes on the Senate floor. He was, however, a good networker and made many friends and political supporters while in Washington. He served in the Senate until his election as president in 1920.

During Harding's time in the Senate, he voted in favor of the United States entering World War I and in most of the war-related legislation, including those that gave additional power to the Democratic president and those that restricted the civil liberties of U.S. citizens. During the war, Harding served on the Senate Foreign Relations Committee. He eventually came around to supporting women's suffrage and, despite drinking alcohol himself, voted for the Eighteenth Amendment, which established the prohibition of alcohol. After the war, Harding came out against President Wilson's plan for the

Warren G. Harding in his golf clothes with a dog, circa 1915–23. *Photograph by Harris & Ewing. Library of Congress, Prints and Photographs Division.*

Warren G. Harding speaking to a campaign rally crowd from the front porch of his home in Marion, Ohio, 1920. *Courtesy of the Ohio History Connection (P146_B20P14_002).*

League of Nations, an international peacekeeping organization that was formed at the end of World War I. Wilson wanted the United States to join the League, but Harding and other Republicans argued that the United States should not be obligated to entangle itself in European politics.

Harding continued to play an important role in Republican and Ohio politics and was asked to give the keynote speech at the 1916 Republican National Convention. Four years later, Harding decided to run for president himself. By the 1920 election season, sixteen states were holding presidential primaries in advance of the official Republican National Convention. Harding was not a clear frontrunner after the primaries or in the first day of voting at the convention. After some back-room dealings that evening, Harding emerged as the Republican nominee by the tenth round of balloting. He selected Massachusetts governor Calvin Coolidge as his running mate. Their Democratic opponent was Ohio governor James Cox, with Franklin D. Roosevelt as his running mate.

Harding's presidential campaign slogan was "A Return to Normalcy," which struck a nerve with Americans recovering from the disruptions of a world war and the recent influenza epidemic. Harkening back to the successful campaigns of his Ohio predecessors, Harding planned a "front porch" presidential campaign, inviting supporters to visit his Marion home rather than traveling the country, as the Democrats commonly did. This would be the last of such front porch campaigns. An estimated 600,000 people made the journey by train to Marion, where they were led by local marching bands through town and to the Harding home. Neighbors reportedly set up concession stands in their front yards to feed the visitors and sell souvenirs. Florence was so concerned about the front yard that she arranged to have tons of gravel placed all over the grass. It was a mostly successful campaign, although by August the Republican Party had begun to second guess themselves, and Harding began giving speeches outside Marion. He was noted as particularly popular with the media, due in large part to his affinity with newspaper reporters.

Election day—November 2, 1920—was Harding's fifty-fifth birthday. On that day, Florence became the first wife to vote for her husband as president. (The Nineteenth Amendment guaranteeing women the right to vote was ratified earlier that year.) Harding won, with the largest landslide victory in Republican history.

PRESIDENCY

Warren G. Harding stepped into a presidency that hadn't paid a lot of attention to domestic affairs in the most recent years. The United States had officially entered World War I in April 1917, not long after Woodrow Wilson began his second term as president. The entire nation was focused on war, and once it ended, Wilson was occupied with negotiating peace abroad and then lobbying for the United States to join the League of Nations. In October 1919, Wilson suffered a debilitating stroke that left him largely incapacitated for the remainder of his presidency, and not much was accomplished for the next eighteen months.

When Harding took office in March 1921, the unity that held the country together during war had largely splintered. Labor unrest was an ongoing concern, and in the spring of 1922, Harding got involved in trying to negotiate the end to a protracted strike by coal miners and railroad workers. He could not get labor and management to reach an agreement and finally authorized his attorney general to file an injunction against the strikers for interrupting mail service and interstate commerce. The injunction ended the strike but damaged the Harding administration's support among laborers. Harding also faced criticism when he vetoed a bill that would have given a bonus to World War I veterans for their service. The bill had support in Congress, but Harding argued that the federal government couldn't afford the billions of dollars that it would cost.

Harding did support legislation that benefited American farmers and encouraged both federal and state governments to pursue public works projects that would give work to returning veterans. He also created a federal department of public welfare and supported the 1921 Federal Highway Act, which funded the construction of a national highway system.

When it came to race relations, Harding had a mixed record. He appointed several African Americans to high-level positions in the federal government but did not go as far as some would have liked. He did speak out in support of racial equality, most notably in a speech he gave in Birmingham, Alabama, where he argued that Black people should have the same political and educational opportunities as whites—a statement that was still very unpopular in the Democrat-dominated South.

During his time in the White House, Harding unified the federal budget for the first time and created the General Accounting Office to provide oversight. Harding also received recognition for calling a conference to reduce naval power, held in Washington in 1921. The Washington Naval War Conference was the first of its kind and convened nine countries to set limits on building warships.

The Hardings had a busy schedule of social entertaining during their years in Washington. Florence enjoyed entertaining and particularly welcomed musicians and celebrities to the White House. Warren liked to play poker, and they both served alcohol to close guests, in defiance of Prohibition.

In early 1923, Harding came down with what was believed at the time to be influenza but may have been a heart attack. Subsequently, he had trouble sleeping and breathing at night. Doctors of the time had only begun to understand heart issues, so there was not much to do other than watch and wait.

The Hardings had been planning a trip to the West Coast and Alaska for the summer of 1923. They proceeded, despite concerns about Warren's health and Florence's lingering kidney problems. They traveled by train to St. Louis, Denver, Salt Lake City and Portland and then took a boat to Alaska. They had a wonderful trip, but on the way home, Harding fell ill. They detoured to a hotel in San Francisco, where Harding's doctor diagnosed him with food poisoning. He was put on bed rest, and over the next few weeks,

Warren and Florence Harding on board the USS *Henderson* during their trip to Alaska, shortly before his death in 1923. *Courtesy of the Ohio History Connection (P146_B37_F12_01).*

it appeared that he was recovering. On August 2, Florence was sitting by his bedside reading to him when Warren suffered what was likely another heart attack and died.

HARDING'S LEGACY

In the years after his death, Warren G. Harding's reputation was tarnished as the public became aware of the scandals—both political and personal—in which he was reputedly involved.

Shortly before Harding's death, the head of his Veterans Bureau was found to be selling surplus federal supplies to private contractors at a steep discount. At the time, Harding confronted him but allowed him to resign without much consequence. It was eventually revealed that the administrator was involved in a much bigger scheme to get kickbacks on land and construction purchases for a new Veterans Administration hospital to the tune of nearly $2 million. Harding is believed not to have known about the extent of the fraud but was later criticized for not taking swifter action to hold a member of his administration accountable for his misdeeds.

The largest of the scandals surrounding Harding came to be known as Teapot Dome. In this scheme, Harding's secretary of the interior, Albert Fall, was caught leasing federal oil reserves in Wyoming to private companies in return for at least $400,000 in bribes. Fall was convicted of bribery and became the first member of a presidential cabinet to serve time in jail. Although Harding was only indirectly involved, and the story didn't break until after his death, Harding's name has remained connected to the scandal.

Harding's personal life was also not above public reproach. Four years after his death, a woman named Nan Britton published a book where she claimed that Harding had fathered her child. The Harding family disputed the claims, but Britton's book was immensely popular at the time. DNA testing in 2015 confirmed a genetic connection between Harding's and Britton's descendants, although some of the more salacious portions of Britton's book are believed to have been exaggerated.

Britton was not Harding's only extramarital paramour. Around 1905, Harding began a years-long affair with one of his wife's closest friends, Carrie Phillips. Florence Harding apparently knew of the affair, although she believed it had ended much sooner than it did. When Harding ran for president, Phillips threatened to expose the love letters he had written to her. He offered her $5,000 per year for her silence, and the Republican National Committee financed a vacation abroad for Phillips and her husband. All this information remained largely out of the public eye until decades later.

Upon Warren's death, Florence asked for his papers to be sent to her in Marion, where she destroyed them. She then died a year later. But in 1929, it was discovered that nearly one hundred cubic feet of papers from his time in the Senate and his presidential campaign had been left in the basement of the White House. Included in those papers were his letters to Carrie Phillips. The records remained with the Harding Memorial Association until the 1960s, when they were finally transferred to the Ohio Historical Society and made available to the public.

WARREN G. HARDING HISTORIC SITES IN OHIO

Warren G. Harding Birthplace
6297 Ohio Route 97, Blooming Grove, Ohio

The house where Warren G. Harding was born is no longer standing. A historical marker identifies the location.

Warren G. Harding Presidential Sites
380 Mount Vernon Avenue, Marion, Ohio
740-387-9630
hardingpresidentialsites.org

The Warren G. Harding Presidential Sites is composed of the Warren G. Harding Presidential Library and Museum and the home that the Hardings lived in from its construction in 1890 until Florence Harding's death in 1924.

The Presidential Library and Museum, the newest of the Ohio presidential sites, was supposed to open to the public on the 100th anniversary of Harding's 1920 presidential campaign. The COVID-19 pandemic postponed the opening to May 2021. The building houses an exhibit gallery that tells the story of the restoration of the Harding Home and a gift shop. Also featured are two videos: one about Warren G. Harding's life that includes archival photos and film footage and another about the archaeological excavations at the site. The museum is self-guided.

The Harding Home is adjacent to the Presidential Library and Museum and is open by guided tour. Warren and Florence had this Queen Anne–style Victorian home built while they were engaged and were married in the entryway in 1891. The couple lived in the house for the next three decades, making only modest improvements, including adding electricity and a big, beautiful wraparound porch in 1903, the latter modeled after the porch on a neighboring home. It was from this porch that Warren launched his "front porch" presidential campaign in 1920.

The house is currently interpreted to that summer of 1920, but this has not always been the case. After Florence Harding's death in 1924, the house and most of its contents were left to the Harding Memorial Association, an organization composed of members of Harding's cabinet, Washington friends and Marion businessmen. The Memorial Association opened the house for tours just two years later. For years, the house was interpreted to

Warren G. Harding Presidential Library and Museum in Marion, Ohio. *Author's collection.*

The home of Warren G. Harding in Marion, Ohio. *Author's collection.*

circa 1900. In the mid-1960s, the Ohio Historical Society (now the Ohio History Connection) took possession of the house, and the restoration completed in 2020 focused on restoring the house to its 1920 appearance, including reproductions of the original wall and floor coverings.

The Harding home is a surprisingly modest four-bedroom, one-bath house just a short walk from what was then the headquarters of the *Marion Star*. (The newspaper still exists; the headquarters building does not.) Almost all the furniture, decorative items and personal things in the house are original and belonged to the Hardings. The guided tour includes all the rooms on the first and second floors of the house, including the bathroom and kitchen. Of particular interest are items including Florence's jewelry box, given to her on her sixteenth birthday; barrister cases with family books; and a portrait painting of one of the family dogs hung above the mantel in the library. Also of note are the original fixtures, including sinks with three faucets—hot, cold and cistern—and buckeye-themed stained-glass windows.

Also on the Harding property is a small kit house that was constructed in just two days during the 1920 presidential campaign and used by reporters covering the campaign. The house was built in the backyard of the Hardings' next-door neighbor; they also rented out their house for the Republican Party to use as headquarters for the summer.

The Warren G. Harding Presidential Sites are open daily, and an admission is charged.

The Harding Memorial
Intersection of Vernon Heights Boulevard and Delaware Avenue, Marion, Ohio

After Warren G. Harding's sudden death in San Francisco in 1923, his body was returned via train to Ohio, where it was temporarily interred in the local cemetery while the Harding Memorial Association raised money for a permanent memorial. It took about two years to raise the funds needed to build the memorial—all from private funds—and another year to complete the marble memorial. Warren and Florence were interred there in December 1927.

The memorial is located on a small rise on a ten-acre plot of land adjacent to the town cemetery. The memorial, believed to be the largest one outside Washington, D.C., was designed by a Pittsburgh architectural firm after a nationwide competition. The Harding Memorial is open dawn to dusk and is free.

Warren G. Harding Memorial in Marion, Ohio. *Author's collection.*

Historic Harding Cabin
22300 State Park Road 20, Mount Sterling, OH
740-869-2020
deercreekparklodge.com/lodging/harding-cabin

Warren G. Harding's presidential retreat is now part of Deer Creek Lodge and Conference Center, a resort in Mount Sterling, Ohio. The cabin is available for overnight lodging.

BIBLIOGRAPHY

Barnard, Harry. *Rutherford B. Hayes and His America.* New York: Russell & Russell, 1967.

Boomhower, Ray E. *Mr. President: A Life of Benjamin Harrison.* Indianapolis: Indiana Historical Society Press, 2018.

Bunting, Josiah, III. *Ulysses S. Grant.* New York: Times Books, 2004.

Calhoun, Charles W. *Benjamin Harrison.* New York: Times Books, 2005.

Dean, John W. *Warren G. Harding.* New York: Times Books, 2004.

Everett, Marshall. *Complete Life of William McKinley and Story of His Assassination: An Authentic and Official Memorial Edition.* Self-published, 1901.

Gary, Ralph. *The Presidents Were Here: A State-by-State Historical Guide.* Jefferson, NC: McFarland & Company, Inc., Publishers, 2008.

Gutek, Gerald, and Patricia Gutek. *Pathways to the Presidency: A Guide to the Lives, Homes, and Museums of the U.S. Presidents.* Columbia: University of South Carolina Press, 2011.

Hamilton, Neil A. *Presidents: A Biographical Dictionary.* New York: Checkmark Books, 2001.

Kondik, Kyle. *The Bellwether: Why Ohio Picks the President.* Athens: Ohio University Press, 2016.

Korda, Michael. *Ulysses S. Grant: The Unlikely Hero.* New York: Atlas Books, 2004.

Merry, Robert W. *President McKinley: Architect of the American Century.* New York: Simon and Schuster Paperbacks, 2017.

Millard, Candice. *Destiny of the Republic: A Tale of Madness, Medicine and the Murder of a President.* New York: Doubleday, 2011.

Miller, Scott. *The President and the Assassin: McKinley, Terror and Empire at the Dawn of the American Century.* New York: Random House, 2011.

Morris, Ray, Jr. *Fraud of the Century: Rutherford B. Hayes, Samuel Tilden and the Stolen Election of 1876.* New York: Simon and Schuster, 2003.

Painter, Mark P. *William Howard Taft: President and Chief Justice.* Cincinnati, OH: Jarndyce & Jarndyce Press, 2004.

Rohr, David E. *The United States of Ohio: One American State and Its Impact on the Other 49.* Columbus: Ohio State University Press, 2019.

Rutkow, Ira. *James Garfield.* New York: Times Books, 2006.

Smith, Jordan Michael. "The Letters that Warren G. Harding's Family Didn't Want You to See." *New York Times Magazine,* July 7, 2014, 31.

Thomas, Dale. *Ohio Presidents: A Whig and Seven Republicans.* Charleston, SC: Arcadia Publishing, 2019.

Trefousse, Hans L. *Rutherford B. Hayes.* New York: Times Books, 2002.

Weeks, Philip, ed. *Buckeye Presidents: Ohioans in the White House.* Kent: Kent State University Press, 2003.

WEBSITES

Benjamin Harrison Presidential Site. bhpsite.org.

Garfield Trail, Hiram College. hiram.edu/about-hiram-college/history-of-the-college/garfield-trail.

Miller Center, University of Virginia. millercenter.org.

Niles (Ohio) Historical Society. nileshistoricalsociety.org.

Ohio History Connection. ohiohistory.org.

Rutherford B. Hayes Presidential Library and Museum. rbhayes.org.

Ulysses S. Grant National Historic Site. nps.gov/ulsg.

White House Historical Association. whitehousehistory.org.

ABOUT THE AUTHOR

Heather S. Cole is a writer and public historian living in the Shenandoah Valley of Virginia. She has an MA in history and has worked in a variety of museums and archives. Her previous book, *Virginia's Presidents: A History & Guide*, was published by The History Press in 2023. She is currently working on a book about the history of medical museums.

Visit us at
www.historypress.com